The Best
Women's Stage Monologues
of 1993

edited by Jocelyn A. Beard

The Monologue Audition Series

SK
A Smith and Kraus Book

Published by Smith and Kraus, Inc.
Newbury, Vermont
Copyright © 1993 by Smith and Kraus, Inc.
All rights reserved

COVER AND TEXT DESIGN BY JULIA HILL
Manufactured in the United States of America

FIrst Edition: December 1993
10 9 8 7 6 5 4 3 2 1

The Monologue Audition Series ISSN 1067-134X

NOTE: These monologues are intended to be used for audition and class study; permission is not required to use the material for those purposes. However, if there is a paid performance of any of the monologues included in this book, please refer to the permissions acknowledgment pages to locate the source who can grant permission for public performance.

Smith and Kraus *Books For Actors*

THE MONOLOGUE SERIES

The Best Men's/Women's Stage Monologues of 1992
The Best Men's/Women's Stage Monologues of 1991
The Best Men's/Women's Stage Monologues of 1990
One Hundred Men's/Women's Stage Monologues from the 1980's
2 Minutes and Under: Character Monologues for Actors
Street Talk: Character Monologues for Actors
Uptown: Character Monologues for Actors
Monologues from Contemporary Literature: Volume I
Monologues from Classic Plays

FESTIVAL MONOLOGUE SERIES

The Great Monologues from the Humana Festival
The Great Monologues from the EST Marathon
The Great Monologues from the Women's Project
The Great Monologues from the Mark Taper Forum

YOUNG ACTORS SERIES

Great Scenes and Monologues for Children
New Plays from A.C.T.'s Young Conservatory
Great Scenes for Young Actors from the Stage
Great Monologues for Young Actors

SCENE STUDY SERIES

Scenes From Classic Plays 468 B.C. to 1960 A.D.
The Best Stage Scenes of 1993
The Best Stage Scenes of 1992
The Best Stage Scenes for Women from the 1980's
The Best Stage Scenes for Men from the 1980's

PLAYS FOR ACTORS SERIES

Romulus Linney: 17 Short Plays
Eric Overmyer: Collected Plays
Lanford Wilson: 21 Short Plays
William Mastrosimone: Collected Plays
Horton Foote: 4 New Plays
Israel Horovitz: 17 short Plays

GREAT TRANSLATION FOR ACTORS SERIES

The Wood Demon by Anton Chekhov

OTHER BOOKS IN OUR COLLECTION

Humana Festival '93: The Complete Plays
The Actor's Chekhov
Women Playwrights: The Best Plays of 1992
Kiss and Tell: Restoration Scenes, Monologues, & History
Cold Readings: Some Do's and Don'ts for Actors at Auditions

If you require pre-publication information about upcoming Smith and Kraus monologues collections, scene collections, play anthologies, advanced acting books, and books for young actors, you may receive our semi-annual catalogue, free of charge, by sending your name and address to *Smith and Kraus Catalogue, P.O. Box 10, Newbury, VT 05051. (800) 862 5423 FAX (802) 866 5346*

Contents

Introduction

The general audition is most often the actor's pathway to future casting or admission to professional actor-training programs. In the few allotted minutes of the audition, the actor must show personal truth, imagination, talent, and training through *material* that is at once uncommon and provocative.

One of the actor's most constant tasks is finding fresh audition material which will not fall tiresomely upon the director's ear. This has been the actor's chore for 2,500 years, or, since the Ancient Greeks began the system of open auditions for the Festival of Dionysius.

Today, the *general audition* takes place largely for admission to professional actor-training programs, for roles in university and summer theatres, and for casting directors working with stage, film, and television productions. Most directors (and teachers) encounter the same selections over and over again during auditions; therefore, it is vital to present fresh, interesting material. In all instances, the actor must capture our attention with a well-chosen monologue as an expression of personal power, truth, and uniqueness. And, it must be clear that the actor has done so with a clear, comprehensive understanding of the play in its entirety.

The fifty-eight monologues found in *The Best Women's Stage Monologues of 1993* serve the particular needs of actresses looking for fresh material. The editor has provided a range of modern roles addressing diversity, ethnicity, sexual orientation, age, style, and experience. These women's roles are as varied as Lanford Wilson's Asian American pianist in *Redwood Curtain* and Paula Vogel's lesbian mother in *And Baby Makes Seven.* These selections, including works by Larry Kramer, Jane Martin, and Kathleen Tolan from the 1992-93 theatrical season, are eclectic, stylish, and challenging. They provide us with "American" voices as vehicles for realizing our own uniqueness as American actors and for mastering the audition process with challenging material.

This anthology is a valuable source book for the actor's personal library as well as a convenient tool for actors whose search for new and interesting material is never-ending in this business.

Milly S. Barranger
Producing Director
PlayMakers Repertory Company
Chapel Hill, North Carolina

The Best
Women's Stage Monologues
of 1993

ALABAMA RAIN
by Heather McCutcheon

Pheenie, a young woman on a journey, 20s
Setting: here and now
Dramatic

Pheenie has left her dry Alabama home in search of the ocean.
She is eventually drawn to Cocoa Beach in Florida, where she
finally dips her toes into the water.

○　　　○　　　○

PHEENIE: I liked getting my toes wet. Cool and intimate feeling
. . . The water fit around my skin like it was made for me.

I started walking north along the coast and I kept my feet in
the way of the waves the whole time.

I walked all through the night. I saw the sun come up right
as I reached a hard strip of sand called Cocoa Beach.

I stopped to watch the sun rise, and I saw something else.
There was a kind of puff of smoke like in a magic trick, and
then a big streamer of smoke leading up into the sky. Straight
up, breaking free of the Earth, going *that* high. I ran toward it
until the sand gave way to a strip of concrete. A launch pad. It
does just what its name suggests. It launches people. Right up
into space. And guess what? They send people all the way to
the moon.

I tried to get aboard, and they were real nice, but said no.
Not even on the waiting list. It's probably just as well, because
I heard a lot of talk about what they call the splash down.

I was ready to go up. Imagine the view, imagine how far
you could see from up there? You could see past tomorrow
on into next week. Maybe next *year*. I was ready to *see* all
that.

I just wasn't ready to splash down into the middle of it.

Back at home, they were no better off. It was like my poor
sisters kept saying please and thank you and nobody was
saying yes or you're welcome. The balance was gone. All of a
sudden it seemed everything had gone thirsty.

AND BABY MAKES SEVEN
by Paula Vogel

Ruth, a woman whose lover has just had a baby, 30s
Setting: an apartment in Manhattan, the present
Serio-Comic

*Ruth and Anna have wanted a child for a long time. When
Nathan is born, Ruth speaks to his biological father of her love
for Anna and her desire to be a parent.*

○　　　○　　　○

RUTH: He looks just like you. (*Beat.*)

I guess Anna and I really started talking about having a child
after our first year together. You know how it is, that first year
. . . you spend every moment in side glances at your lover,
learning this new alphabet . . . her face, her walk, her gestures
. . . the way she holds a pen, the way she chews the inside of
her cheek in concentration; how her left nostril flairs ever so
slightly when she's amused – and you feel so ardent, you're in
first grade all over again, in love with your teacher – so much
in love that you wake early to study this alphabet while she's
still asleep, memorizing her face on the pillow . . .

And I used to imagine that somewhere in the United States
there must be a pioneer geneticist, a woman in a lab coat we
could go to, who would take some DNA from Anna and some
DNA from me – and she'd combine us in a petri dish in a little
honeymoon culture at just the right temperature – and then
this growing synthesis would be transplanted in one of us, and
when he or she would emerge, nine months later – the baby
would have Anna's eyes winking beneath my eyebrows.

But finally I thought – well, I can always see my own face
anytime I want to in the mirror. But I could see Anna's face at
birth, Anna in diapers, a little Anna coming home from school
– or, if the baby was born a boy, even better – I'd see his
Adam's apple grow beneath her chin, or I'd experience that
painful moment right before puberty, before his voice
changes, when I mistake his hello on the phone for hers –

Well, I guess I didn't think this all the way through.

ANDY FAFIRSIN
by Don Nigro

Alice, a young woman plotting to kill her husband, 18-20
Setting: mythical Tudor England
Dramatic

Alice is driven to thoughts of murder by her desire for Thomas, a servant in her husband's household. Here, she speaks to Thomas of her lonely life.

O   O   O

ALICE: Do you know, Tommy, with what enormous difficulty I often must refrain from screaming, as I move through the basic little domestic tasks of the day? It keeps receding from me, the world does, it runs away from my fingertips, as when it rains. I must be absolutely soaked within the rain or rain is just not real to me. At night sometimes I creep out naked from my bed and go behind the house and smell the woods and wet and look at stars and cry, for I can't touch them with my fingers, I want to feel the dark between me, want the Lord to touch me and rub off my skin.
[**MOSBY:** Alice!]
ALICE: I want, my love, some contact and relation which I fear is just not possible the way my world is so constructed now, do you see? So I must DO something about this, I must reconstruct the world the way I want it, for to make it real again. I need to make it bleed to know it's real. Do you SEE? Do you SEE? Oh, why do you ask me why? You make me sad when you ask why, and you don't want to know the answer anyway. I can't touch you enough, my love, I can't touch anything enough, alas. (*Pause.*) Does that clarify the situation for you, Thomas?

ANDY WARHOL'S SECRET GIRLFRIEND
by Richard Lay

Rosie, Andy Warhol's secret girlfriend, 30s
Setting: NYC & Brooklyn
Serio-Comic

Rosie is a simple Brooklyn gal who works in the garment district. One day she encountered Andy Warhol on a bus and lent him five dollars. A strange romance ensued. Here, Rosie contemplates her first love, a house painter named Boris.

O   O   O

ROSIE: *(To audience.)* Am I the biggest idiot in the world? Andy Warhol loves me and I am his secret girlfriend . . . that should be enough, shouldn't it? Let me say it slowly. ANDY WARHOL loves me. We met on a bus . . . and he says he loves me. Yer see, I've always loved Andy Warhol . . . but it was easier before I knew him. Don't get me wrong . . . To feel his blond wig and limp hands and kiss his uneducated lips are everything. I am in the full flush of accomplishing celebrity Secret Girlfriend status . . . which I have . . . because HE says so . . . But why can't I see him in Manhattan? WHY can't I go clubbing with him? Why can't I be seen on his arm? No man has entered my body because I respect my faith and Andy doesn't even know how to nuzzle or cuddle or kiss . . . I have to ask, will Andy Warhol ever do something with his Secret Girlfriend? Now that I am over Boris Sullivan and am still a Virgin . . . I have a right to challenge Andy to a physical relationship . . . I had a dream about Boris last night and he was the Tsar of Russia . . . *(Slower.)* I guess I shouldn't have told him he was an Almost Man to his face. I could see the hurt in his eyes. When I said it I meant it . . . Do you think it was easy for me not to get married on my wedding day? . . . Poppa insisted that the wedding reception should go on because he'd paid for the band. My eyes kept going towards the door, just in case Boris would look in and tell me he understood. Did I even understand? I danced with all my uncles and cousins and the band played wedding tunes

4

because that's all they knew. We made the best of a disaster and everybody smiled and ate cake. Nobody said I had done the wrong thing . . . Nobody . . . All I could think of was Boris crying. He had pleaded with me to change my mind and I had found a certain pleasure in holding my ground and seeing his pain . . . The troubling thing is, that's not like me at all. When he called me a Jewish Princess, at that very moment, I knew he knew he couldn't win . . . Andy's coming over tonight. I told him we had to talk – secretly!

ANTIGONE IN NEW YORK
by Janusz Glowacki

Anita, a homeless Puerto Rican, 30-40
Setting: Thompson Square Park, NYC
Dramatic

Here, good-hearted Anita tells the story of how she came to be homeless.

○   ○   ○

ANITA: (*Showing him the label.*) See? It's sewn with white thread. Calvin Klein would never do that. The knot is very sloppy and unprofessional. I know about these things because I worked in a sweat shop with my mother. After we came to this country. We were very lucky to get those jobs. I made thirty-five cents per coat lining but my mother got forty-five because she was so fast and she took work home. We'd work sometimes eighteen hours a day. We were saving to go back to Puerto Rico as soon as possible. We wanted to buy a little bodega, you know, a little grocery store, which would have blue and red lights blinking all around the door. Beautiful like a Christmas tree or those police car lights, the ones that go around and around. So everything is blue and then red and then blue and then red. So pretty. My mother was dreaming that one day my father, who ran away with another woman, would walk in our bodega and he would stare in astonishment at what we had. Then my mother would walk out of the back and show herself proudly to him. And she'd say "it's me. I did all this and there's nothing for you." And the lights would be blinking and he would fall on his knees and beg her and plead with her to come back to him, to let him work for her, anything but she would just turn around and walk out and slam the door. And then she and my brother and me would laugh and laugh and laugh and he would have to go back to that bitch with nothing in his hands.

6

APPROXIMATING MOTHER
by Kathleen Tolan

Molly, a mother-to-be, 30s
Setting: NYC, the present
Serio-Comic

Just days away from her due date, Molly tells her best friend of the trouble that she has been having with her husband.

O   O   O

MOLLY: He told me the other night I never loved him.
   [**FRAN:** What?!]
MOLLY: I was telling him how Jimmy had told me *he* feels like *Doreen* doesn't really love *him,* they never, like, spontaneously hop into bed, it always has to be planned, and he doesn't feel she's reacting to *him, exactly,* and Jack says, well, that's how I feel about you. I've never felt you really love me. And I say, what are you talking about? How could you feel this? You've always felt this and never told me? You've just been living this lie, sleeping beside me every night? And I just lose it. And he calls me a lunatic, says only *I* am so convoluted that I would consider *me* not loving *him his* betrayal. Which in a way makes sense I guess but at the time I felt, Christ, I couldn't sleep beside him for one night much less six years thinking he didn't really love me and didn't he care?
   [**FRAN:** Jesus. Why do I want to get married? That's the real mystery.]
MOLLY: So I'm completely hysterical. And he says, see, someone else would've said something reassuring like of course I love you, but *you* – it's all about *you,* isn't it. Methinks thou doth protest too much. And I really think he's driving me crazy. I thought he hadn't been making love to me because he's a fattist which is kind of despicable if you focus on it but most people are that way and really if you focus on every little thing you really will just stop.
   [**FRAN:** (*Thinking about herself.*) Right]
MOLLY: Just stop.
   [**FRAN:** Yeah.]

MOLLY: So I thought, don't get upset about it, it'll pass, this is just a temporary condition, of course wishing he was one of those guys who was completely into the whole thing, you know? Who get completely turned on by their wive's ripening, marvel at the miracle –

[**FRAN:** Good luck.]

MOLLY: Right. Anyway, I just couldn't get up the next morning. Jack got up with Jane who had a fit, came sobbing into the bedroom begging me to get up but I just couldn't and she refused to go to school and Jack got the babysitter to come and I just lay in bed crying all day. Finally, Irene had to leave so I got up and went in and lay on the couch and Jane gave me this really strange look and I said, "I was sick. But now I'm better." And she smiled this kind of fake smile and said, "Oh." And I said, "Were you worried about me?" And she said, "Yes, I thought you were going to die of sadness."

APPROXIMATING MOTHER
by Kathleen Tolan

Jen, a pregnant teen
Setting: Indiana, the present
Serio-Comic

Jen tells of her visit to a social worker to discuss her accidental pregnancy.

○   ○   ○

JEN: And said she'd help me and wouldn't tell my parents so I went to her and she told me I would regret it if I had an abortion and I said I regretted this whole thing but that's what I wanted to do and I didn't want to have a baby, I wanted to finish high school and stuff and she said if I wasn't ready to be a mother there were many wonderful couples who would love a baby and I said, well that's fine but I don't want to do that so she said I needed to have permission from my parents and then I should come back to her and she'd help me but I should think about how I'd feel if my parents had decided not to have me and I said, "Huh?" And she said she knew this must be a very scary and confusing time for me and I should know she was my friend and I said I didn't think so and then she got really nasty because she knew I could see right through her and she started screeching, "Go ahead, kill the baby. Kill the baby. See how it makes you feel." And some day I'd wish I had a baby, wouldn't I and I said I don't know what you're talking about, let me out of here and went home and went up to my room and was just shaking and crying and I told my mom I had the flu and just stayed up there for a couple of days and finally I told my mom I was pregnant. And then everybody completely freaked out and here I am.

BIG TIM AND FANNY

by Jack Gilhooley and Daniel Czitrom

Kathleen, a brash young woman, 18-20
Setting: New York City – the night of the fire at the Triangle
Shirtwaist Factory
Dramatic

*Here, a young girl with street smarts offers an eyewitness
account of the horrific fire at the Triangle Shirtwaist Factory.*

O   O   O

KATHLEEN: *(To the audience.)* I knew a number of them from
the neighborhood. Lotsa greenhorns. Mostly Jewish . . . some
Italian. Mostly women. No, make that . . . girls. I saw the fire
escape collapse on the Greene Street side. It was the weight
of the people plus the flames meltin' the iron. Some tumbled
right off and straight down. Others hung on until the flames
got them. One girl clung to the fire escape and held her sister
by the wrist . . . danglin' out there in space. Then the one let
go and they plunged eight floors . . . hand-in-hand. I said to
myself, "Jesus, Mary and Joseph." Not cursin'. Implorin'. A
young girl named Katzstein who lived down the street . . . she
was the only one I seen who fell an' then got up. Despite
everythin' horrible that we'd been seein', we all broke out in
tears an' shouts of joy. I figgered she was about fourteen an' I
remembered that children could sometimes take a fall cause
their bodies weren't so brittle. She got up an' staggered about
two feet . . . then dropped over dead.
(Beat.)
I guess she wasn't young enough.

BIG TIM AND FANNY

by Jack Gilhooley and Daniel Czitrom

Esther, a young Jewish immigrant, 18-20
Setting: New York City – the night of the fire at the Triangle
Shirtwaist Factory
Dramatic

*Esther, an employee of the Triangle Shirtwaist Company, was
fortunate enough to have escaped the fire. Here, she tells her
story.*

O   O   O

ESTHER: I vas a sleevemaker. I escaped vitout a problem. I vas
one of d'first out. I vorked on d'sevent'. I vaited for my fodder
to come down from d'eight. Soon I realized how severe vas
d'fire. I tried to run back inside but d'firemen, d'ey stopped
me. I'd get hit by a falling body or get boined. I cried. I said to
myself, "Americans don't die in fires." I only spoke Yiddish
d'en but I heard of d'is place called a morgue. Only I vas afraid
to go. Afraid of what I might find. I got on a train an' vent
home. I got off at a hundred an' sixteent'. I ran to a hundred
an' nineteent'. I cried all d'vay. V'en I got to d'door of
d'apartment, a strange t'ing happened. I relaxed. I vent in. My
mudder greeted me, said my fodder hadn't arrived yet. I says,
"Yeah, he musta got overtime." I said I vas goin' down
t'd'stoop. But I ran back t'd'train. I vas goin' t'd'morgue. I vas
about t'get onna downtown v'en I looked across an' saw him
get offa d'uptown. He vas filthy . . . bloody . . . shirtless. D'is
most dignified of men people looked at like he vas a bum. Vit'
my last strengt' I shouted across an' vent tearin' over d'liddle
bridge separatin' d'platforms. Ve fell inta each udder's arms.
People stared vhile I hugged an' kissed d'bum over an' over.

BORN GUILTY
by Ari Roth
Based on the book by Peter Sichrovsky

Sibylle, the daughter of a Nazi, 40s
Setting: Germany, the present
Dramatic

Writer Peter Sichrovsky is in the process of researching a book on the children of Nazis. Here he interviews Sibylle, who describes the brutal fascism with which she was raised.

O   O   O

SIBYLLE: My father once told me that he was never given anything he wanted as a child. For example, he wanted to have a raspberry soda with his meals. As a matter of principle, he never got it. That was the family way. Not that my brothers and I didn't receive . . . *Beatings* were routine, again, in the time-honored practice. If I tore my dress, a beating. Poor marks, a beating. If I talked back to my parents . . .

I remember growing up, Sunday School, hearing the story of Abraham and Isaac. I didn't react the way the other kids did. It never struck me as strange that a father would tie his child to a rock because someone had told him to. You see, I thought parents had a *right* to kill their children.

When I was sixteen, I went to Sachsenhausen. I came home and told my mother what I'd seen. Her comment: "The things you do to yourself . . . " That same year, I gave them a book. In it, the author mentions a doctor. Well, it seems my parents *knew* this doctor and, according to them, the day the book places him in the camp, he wasn't there at all. But at our house, delivering one of my brothers. Which was all the proof they needed to know that "this six million" wasn't all it was cracked up to be.

The crowning touch was their cynicism in naming me Sibylle, so that my initials would always be "S.S." One of my father's little jokes.

My brothers say they never had a problem with him and, the fact is, it is difficult to charge Father with anything specific.

By sheer accident, it seems he was never present when anything horrendous was happening. He sailed through his de-Nazification. Still, he remained a fascist to his dying day. You can't imagine . . . Once my older brother was supposed to memorize a poem. Every time he stumbled Father . . . I can still hear the screams. Mother took me by the hand. "Father's going to kill Erich. We better leave." She actually said those words.

CRUISING CLOSE TO CRAZY

by Laura Cunningham

Carolee, a Country Western star suffering from a broken heart, 30s
Setting: the bedroom on a Country Western band's tour bus, the present
Serio-Comic

Carolee's heart has been broken, her voice is all but shot and now she's expected to do a show. Here she describes her plight.

O   O   O

CAROLEE: *(Speaking non-stop, with broken energy.)*
My mouth's so dry, I can't talk.
(Accelerating.)
Nine times in the hospital this year. Nodes. Ain't supposed to sing, that's how come I'm on the road, doing two shows a night, in thirty-six cities. I got letters from doctors all over the world, say, "Carolee, don't sing, don't speak, don't even open your mouth." There's one doctor so big, he's too big for the Mayo Clinic, that's how big he is – took one look down my throat and said, "Don't even open your mouth for a year, Carolee, don't speak, even to *me.*"
(Pause.)
So I kind of nodded at him, then went right back on the road. I can't *do* my people that way. God respects you when you work, but he loves you when you sing.
(She roots through the piled bedding.)
Where's my nerve pills?
(She finds a baggie, pops a pill.)
I thank God I'm not on dope.
(She swallows a few more pills.)
This is just Percodan, for my back.
(She takes another one.)
Clears your head real good, too. I just had a sharp thought.
(She blinks.)
It was passing through.
(She shakes her head, woozily.)

Well, it'll come back. Always *do.*
(*She gropes along the vanity shelf, accidentally knocks off one styrofoam head. Re: her wig.*)
Didn't like that one much, anyway. I had another kind of nerve pill, it was better than most. It was the only one could stop my bad dreamin'.
(*She squints at the audience.*)
You ever dream you was dead? And it was so real, you was surprised to find you wasn't? Only you wake up, it ain't that different?
(*She shivers.*)
I been having dreams so bad, I can't sleep. I'm afraid to put down my head, that's the truth.
(*Shudder.*)
I was wearing my violet dress, I was in a wine-color coffin, in a wine-color room. Everybody in the business come pay their respects. They was all around me, whispering . . .
(*Dull look.*)
But they was drinking beer and eating chicken legs, too. Earl Wayne. Norbie. The Duker . . . Honey Bascomb. They was all there, saying how great I was, but it was a bunch a bull. They were all just thinking: "Now, she's dead, even her old albums will sell."
(*Thoughtful.*)
Well, it worked for Elvis. He gone gold.
(*Sigh.*)
I had to lay there, listening to all their bull, like they wasn't the ones put me right where I was. And they were saying . . .
(*Imitation simper.*)
"Oh, don't she look beautiful, ain't she finally at peace."
(*Militant hiss.*)
Meanwhile, they got the new album piled up outside the funeral home door. Too bad I can't get out of my coffin to sign them.
(*Sweeter, sadder.*)
And you know, the entire time, the entire time, I'm just laying there, waiting for him to come in.
(*She squints at audience.*)
And you know which one. There's only one ever really makes you crazy.

(*Pause as she reflects.*)
Oh, there's some can get you going, make you a little nuts, but there's only one, can *kill* you.
(*Beat.*)
And don't you know? He don't even *show*. He done me dead, like he done me alive.
(*Angry.*)
And now they want me standing next to him in the auditorium lined up with all a them, so we can be the Cavalcade a Fools . . . I can just see it. Him and me, crowned fools a country music, salutin' to our own stupidity. Winding up with Amazin' Grace.
(*Croaking lyrics.*)
"Oh, I'll fly away . . . "
(*Bitter.*)
I'll fly away, all right. I've flown.
(*She shudders.*)
I'm dying. This old bus is going to be my hearse. I'm dying, and there's nobody to care.

CUTE BOYS IN THEIR UNDERPANTS
GO TO FRANCE
by Robert Coles

Dominatrix, a devilish ghoul, 30-40
Setting: an otherwordly S&M classroom
Serio-Comic

*Once condemned for witchcraft, this angry spirit now gives
instruction in the art of sexual torture.*

O   O   O

DOMINATRIX: *(To someone in the first row whom she's chosen:)*
What are you lookin' at?
(Pause. She returns to the main audience.)
I didn't choose to come to this point in my existence. It
wasn't easy being a woman who was in touch with her
sexuality. Not at that time. Oh sure, now we've had the sexual
revolution and all that crap, but I'm talkin' before that. *Way*
before that. When women were supposed to keep their minds
empty and their legs cemented shut. I knew what *I* wanted,
but what a price I had to pay for wanting it! Oy! But that's all
water under the bridge now. Now I'm a supernatural being.
That's what happens to ya if you die with a lot of bitterness
and frustration – you become a supernatural being. I bet you
didn't know that. Well, it's true. And then you get to do what
supernatural beings are meant to do – get revenge! It's true! If
you're filled with this venomous rage, and you're still holding
it in when you die a horrible and unjustified death, you get to
let loose with the venom for the rest of eternity. It's true! You
know, the unseen world is literally crammed full of
supernatural beings, just like me, all of us spending all of our
time getting revenge on living people. It makes sense when
you think about it. Why do you think everybody's life is so
fucked up *all the time?* It's us!
God, how I wish that I'd been able to get back at the same
men who'd abused me, but that was against the rules.
Something about evil not being repaid with evil. In your mortal
life, you're supposed to be able to get away with whatever

despicable shit you can manage to get away with. Doesn't seem fair, does it? But I guess that's the point. You get a free ride for the harm *you* do but you pay for the sins of others.

So we have to victimize strangers. But I still enjoy it. As long as they're men. As long as they're selfish and vain and deeply absorbed in their own genitals. Even if they're gay. I mean, what's the diff? Men are men. These four are pretty much the same as the straight guys I fucked.

We especially enjoy bringing agony to people in show business. It's so easy.

You know, sometimes I think back to those days when I was still alive. I really should have had a grand time, because I knew who I was and I knew it was within my power to make myself happy, and you couldn't say that about very many women in those days.

But that sort of freedom was a forbidden thing back then. For women. As proscribed by men. The same men who enjoyed me in their beds condemned me in the light of day.

Oh, I could have lived with it just fine if it was merely scorn. Big deal. Wear some big red letter on my dress or something. Who gives a fuck. No, it wasn't enough just to brand a woman as a slut. If you were sexual, you were evil. Demonic. Men imagined that you held the devil within you. As if only Satan could make a woman want to have sex with them. Just shows you how neurotic they are about anything that involves their dicks.

So they said I was a witch. Funny, they still call women that these days – it means anyone who's strong and they can't control. Same thing back then. I frightened them.

They thought that fire purified. It doesn't. It just obliterates.

Anyway . . .

(*She pulls herself out of the memories of the past.*)

It's time to get back to *my* favorite hobby – hellish torment.

DAVID'S MOTHER
by Bob Randall

Sally, a woman who has sacrificed everything for her
handicapped son, 40s
Setting: an apartment in New York City, the present
Dramatic

*Sally has struggled for years to keep David out of an institution.
Pursued by guilt and a relentless social worker, she has finally
come to accept the fact that he would be better off in a
program geared to his special needs. Here, Sally tells David of
her decision.*

O   O   O

SALLY: Come on, sweetheart. Nothing bad is happening. Shh.
Come on, calm down. That's a good boy. Cam down. (*He
starts to whimper. His struggling subsides.*) We've got to talk,
sweetheart. I've got to talk and you've got to do your best to
listen. (*He continues to calm.*) Try to listen, honeybunch. (*She
strokes him, he sighs and falls silent.*) I want you to go with
Gladys. I know, I promised you wouldn't have to. But I was
wrong. Things stink around here. They have for a long time. I
just got a whiff of the stench. It's not your fault, sweetheart.
It's mine. (*She strains for the truth.*) You see, in my whole life,
I was never special. I was never pretty enough, or smart
enough or talented enough to be anything but ordinary. And
then you came along and you were the way you were. And I
was the only one who could handle you. Do you have any idea
how special that can make a person feel? You know you're a
piece of work just like me. I could get you up in the morning
and get you dressed and fed and happy. I could make you
happy. So I kept it that way. For me. Not for you. I kept us
here watching movies. And I stayed special. And you stayed
calm. But you know something? Being calm isn't all there is.
There's a whole world out there, David. Even for you. Hey, you
can work a VCR! So I want you to go with Gladys. Let's see
what other tricks you've got up your sleeve. Because the truth
is, I may not be special at all, but you sure as hell are!

THE DESTINY OF ME
by Larry Kramer

Rena, a woman devoted to her youngest son, 30-40
Setting: Autumn, 1992, just outside Washington, DC
Dramatic

Here, Rena tells her son the sad and horrifying tale of her miscarriage.

○   ○   ○

RENA: I'd gone to spend the night with Mother Sybil. She terrified me, too. She was a mean, unloving, self-centered . . . bitch. Grandma Sybil only had one bed. I had to sleep with her. Oh, her smells! Her old-lady unguents and liniments. Don't open the window. I feel a draft. I feel a draft. She started talking to me in the dark. Telling me how much she'd loved him. Her husband. When they first came to America they scrubbed floors together. They'd meet in the middle and kiss. I don't know why but I thought that was very romantic. Then one day someone told her he was cavorting with a lady in Atlantic City. She didn't even let him pack. She said her heart was still broken. She fell asleep crying. I kept waking up. I had to go to the toilet. I tiptoed in the dark. I didn't even flush. I was terrified I'd disturb her. The third or fourth time I smelled a bad smell. Like something spoiled or rotten. The fifth time I turned on the light. The toilet bowl was filled with blood. And lumps of stringy fibers. Like liver. Pieces of raw liver. From the butcher. I was so sleepy. The doctor had given me something to sleep. Why was liver coming out of me? And this awful smell? I went back to her bed. I had to go to the toilet again. And again. By morning I must have been close to death. She demanded her tea in bed. I pulled myself to the kitchen. I fell on the floor in a heap. What must have saved me was the kettle whistling. I couldn't reach up to turn it off. Where's my tea? What's wrong with you, girl? You can't even make my tea. I woke up in the hospital. I'd had a miscarriage. So you see how much I wanted you. Can't you? Can't you see how much I want you?

DOWN THE SHORE
by Tom Donaghy

Luke, a street-smart yet vulnerable teenager, 15
Setting: on the street next to a church outside of Philadelphia,
the present
Serio-Comic

Luke (really Lucy) is pregnant. Here, she tells her story to her long-lost brother, MJ.

O   O   O

LUKE: Phippsey and I didn't know we were making it.

[**MJ:** Making what?]

LUKE: A rug rat. A kid. Not going to fat girl camp. Sal Sal thought some of my baby fat was coming back cause I was about to have another growth spurt. Then told her the fat's due to on accounta I'm about to have a baby spurt. Thought it was pretty funny when the lady at the clinic told me, so I laughed. She didn't think it was as funny as I thought it was. Phippsey thought it was really upchuck funny when I told him, then after awhile it didn't seem, seemed more like, really only was giggling after awhile. Then kinda stopped talking altogether. Only started to look preggers now. And it's cool cause school just ended. So Sal Sal's – telling everyone I'm going to fat girl camp. It's what she's telling them. Cause Hoy said he wouldn't have it in his house on accounta he's a good Catholic. He's moving in tomorrow. His house tomorrow. He's always over going on about we don't have enough dough for a kid. Ha, if he got a job, you know?

[**MJ:** . . . yeah.]

LUKE: So they're driving me down to Aunt Meg Callaghan's tomorrow. Scenic Baltimore. Got the largest aquarium in the country, Sal Sal says. So big you can walk down into it cause they got a staircase in a tube and you can walk down into it and the sharks swim by. After they drop me off they're going on their honeymoon. Then the nuns get the kid. Then I come back at the end of the summer all skinny and ready for junior year. Get your high school picture taken junior year, know that?

FREAKMAKERS
by Jocelyn Beard

The Doctor, a woman in a coma, 40s
Setting: a head trauma ward; late at night
Dramatic

When a neurosurgeon runs afoul of a bullet, she is placed in the same head trauma ward that she once managed. Now her consciousness wanders from memory to memory. Here, her mind pays a visit to a patient that she had once found to be particularly disturbing.

O   O   O

THE DOCTOR: So cold . . . Sometimes . . . sometimes I forget where I am, you know? It's so cold and dark in this place; this night gallery. Rod Serling himself couldn't have . . . What was I saying? (*She turns back to Bed 2.*) How can you stand it?

How can you stand your mother reading you Monty Python day in and day out? How can you stand the nurses touching you, washing you, moving you? Your little girlfriend stopped coming weeks ago, didn't she? It's okay, she wasn't much to jump and shout about . . . well, Dr. Loomis thought so, but he's totally out, if you know what I mean. Comes with the territory: being out. Neurology is as far out as it gets, kid. Or, in your case, in. It's all in there, isn't it? Every fucking answer to every fucking question I've ever asked. Christ. I hate you. (*Studying the bed.*) Hmmm . . . now that the facial lacerations have healed, you've become my most beautiful patient. One might say that your face is . . . unflawed marble in this moonlight. How's that for poetry? Pretty lousy, right? There's still a world out there, kiddo, waiting for you to get back to it. Your beauty is wasted in here. In the night gallery. God, I just hate that you're someplace that I can't get to. You don't deserve it and I'll tell you why: you're too fucking stupid. How in hell did you spend 18 years on this particular planet without figuring out that a bottle of Jack Daniels plus a decked-out Mustang equals bullshit? Oh, I'm not preaching at you, kiddo. Uh-uh. I don't give a shit if people drink until their livers blow bile. At least when I drink, and boy do I drink, I do it at home so I can pass out on my nice, safe bed.

(*Lights up on Remy.*)

Not that my bed was always safe.

GOODNIGHT DESDEMONA
(GOOD MORNING JULIET)
by Ann-Marie MacDonald

Constance, an assistant professor of Renaissance drama, 20-30
Setting: Queens University, the present
Serio-Comic

For years, Constance has devoted herself to the selfish Professor Night. She is shocked when he announces that he is: A.) marrying a young student; B). taking the position that Constance desired for herself at Oxford, and C.) getting her a job at an isolated college on the Canadian prairie.

O   O   O

CONSTANCE: Regina. I hate the prairies. They're flat. It's an absolute nightmare landscape of absolutes and I'm a relativist, I'll go mad. Diamonds are a girl's best friend. Diamonds are harder than a bed of nails. I can't feel anything. I'm perfectly fine. I'll call the Dean and resign. I'll go back to my apartment and watch the plants die and the cats copulate freely. I'll order in groceries. Eventually I'll be evicted. I'll smell really bad and swear at people on the subway. Five years later I run into Professor Night and Roman: they don't recognize me. I'm selling pencils. They buy one. Suddenly, I drop dead. They discover my true identity. I'm awarded a doctorate posthumously. Professor Night dedicates his complete works to me and lays roses on my grave every day. My stone bears a simple epithet: 'Oh what a noble mind is here o'erthrown.' . . . There's no time to lose! I have to start right now if I'm going to sink that low in five years. (*Grabs the phone, dials.*)

HI-ROLLERS
by Jack Gilhooley

Torchy, a young dancer/waitress, 20s
Setting: Rocco's Pussycat Lounge, Las Vegas
Serio-Comic

Torchy will do anything to promote her career as a singer/songwriter; including working at Rocco's Pussycat Lounge.

○   ○   ○

TORCHY: (*At ease.*) Evening, boys, and welcome to Rocco's Pussycat Lounge. Not exactly situated in the heart of Las Vegas, if there is such a thing. More like its guts . . . its loins . . . its entrails. So, what's that make us, huh? (*Beat.*) Hey, only kiddin', guys. (*To the camera.*) You too, Rocco. This is the soooooooul of the city. You're the homeboys . . . the long-haulers . . . the marathoners. No hi-rollers, here. No limos pull up to Rocco's door. And no egg farmers from Peoria with their life's savings. We're the folks on the edge of The Strip . . . the cutting edge . . . the center of the crater. No plastic, implanted kewpie doll showgirls in Rocco's stable. And stable it is! No, we're natural women, through and through . . . top to bottom . . . inside out . . . upside down. And we love you 'cause you never fail to leave a nice gratuity before you stumble out the door. That's "gratuity" as in tip. Not like those tight-fisted, tight-assed polyester cowboys in the lounges. You guys are just like us. Live hard, play hard, leave a good-lookin' corpse. We're the angle players. No marks in here. Or suckers. Well, I'll retract that last comment. Everything has its price. None of us are scared or spooked or freaked by Vegas. 'Cause we got each other. So, give the girls a big reception. And get ready to flash your long green. I'm not referring to the Martian at the bar. You put that long green of yours back in your pants right now, E.T. The nerve. This is a family establishment. And we are famillllly!

HOMEWARD BOUND
by Eliot Hayes

Bonnie, a woman whose husband has just died, 60s
Setting: a living room, the present
Dramatic

Bonnie and Glen have gathered their family together to announce that Glen is dying of an incurable disease and intends to take his own life. When he dies, Bonnie goes into shock.

○   ○   ○

BONNIE: Wouldn't it be funny if he died of natural causes? Well it wouldn't be "funny," but it would be funny. Wouldn't it?

Are you crying, Norris?

I suppose it would be fair to say that I'm in shock. Not that I'm incoherent. I know what I'm saying. After all, I'm prepared for this. Well, not this specifically, but this generally. I'm only surprised, of course, because at least if he had killed himself, I would have been able to say what I wanted to say.

Like in the movies, Norris. (*Beat.*)

In India, a good wife jumps on her husband's funeral pyre. Here, a good wife sends his clothes to the Salvation Army and doesn't date for at least three months. (*Beat.*)

If he were a Pharaoh, though, I'd be buried alive with him in his pyramid to cook his breakfast on the other side. But that's only marginally more civil than jumping on his pyre, if you ask me. Which of course you wouldn't, because it wouldn't be right. And we're all alright here.

At least, though, that way there's some resolution. So you're not just hanging there – in grief, in love, in shock – confused – whatever – thinking about it . . . hoping some convention will hold you in check until it's over, and then wondering if it really was the end. Is the end. "The end," like in your movie, Norris. The end.

THE HOPE ZONE
by Kevin Heelan

Countess, a larger-than-life woman, 50-60
Setting: an AA meeting
Serio-Comic

*Countess has waged a long and successful war against alco-
holism. Here, she addresses her AA group.*

O   O   O

COUNTESS: Well some time past that I had a baby. And it turned
up a baby boy. And raise it I did with love but with liquor too.
And so, one afternoon, with a screamin' sun but a whisperin'
breeze, I fell to sleep for but a breath and my darlin' fell to
sleep but forever. The last thing I shall see as I lay fadin' and
soft shall be his bent brown legs and summer feet kickin' the
sand onto my eyelids as my head, heavy as my heart shall
always be, sinks to the soft cotton warmed by the burnt sand
beneath it. Then, a thousand years, or ten seconds later,
shouts, screams, and sleep. Every night I say a prayer, a selfish
prayer, as most prayers are, I say, "God, tell me that as he
sank to the ocean floor, tell me that as Neptune feasted, he
cried out for mercy, or cursed the world for this trick, or
exploded with the sudden terror, but, God in heaven, tell me
that he did not call out my name. Send a spear through my
skull, invade my every cell with poison from every witch that
ever snarled from every corner, take all that is mine and turn it
to tumbleweed, but tell me that he did not cry, "mother" on
his final afternoon. But God, in his wisdom, stays silent. He
lets us do the talkin'. Right here. Every day the week. If you're
stayin', we got cookies with coffee. If you're leavin', don't get
hungry and don't get lonely. And if you do, pick up a phone
or whack on a door. It's wonderful to see you. God bless you
and keep you and let's get on to cookies with coffee, come
on . . .

IN STITCHES

by Brian Christopher Williams

Mona, a young mother who has lost her son to AIDS, 20-30
Setting: a quilting bee for the Names Quilt Project, the present
Dramatic

*Mona has become involved with the Names Quilt Project in order
to help deal with the death of her son. Here, she shares a special
memory of her little boy with her fellow quilters.*

O   O   O

MONA: People are always doing crazy things on those
commercials and they look so . . . free, I guess . . . but, when I
react, when I . . . it doesn't make me feel good. Once, when
he was staying in the hospital, he was the only child in this
isolated ward that was just for patients with AIDS. I came to
the hospital to pick him up and take him home. He had had a
bad bout, but was feeling a lot better, and when I went to his
room, he wasn't there. And then, I reacted. I started throwing
things, tearing the sheets off his bed and yelling. Yelling all
kinds of things. I stormed down the hallway, looking for a
nurse or somebody; anybody to yell at. Then, I heard Todd
laughing. I couldn't believe my ears. I turned toward his
laughter, and I could hear him telling the story of "The Little
Engine that Could." That was his favorite story. I read it to him
hundreds of times. He would sit on my lap and follow along
with the pictures, and I guess after all those readings he had
memorized it. When I turned the corner and entered the
patient's room, I saw Todd sitting on this man's bed. The man
was lying back on pillows, just so weak, tubes coming out of
his nose and his arms, his face covered with . . . and there,
sitting right next to him was Todd, reading to him "I think I
can, I think I can, I think I can," and then Todd laughed. And
every time Todd laughed, the corners of this man's mouth
would lift, barely noticeable, but they would just sort of lift.
Here was my little sweetheart, my brave little man, not old
enough to care what was expected of him, doing more for
this stranger than I had been doing for my own son. Here, I

had been ashamed of him, when it should have been the other way around.

IN STITCHES
by Brian Christopher Williams

Mrs. Cavendish, a feisty senior citizen, 60-70
Setting: a quilting bee for the Names Quilt Project, the present
Serio-Comic

Mrs. Cavendish has donated the use of her basement to a group that makes panels for the Names Quilt Project. An evening of quilting and discussion has led to speculations about the hereafter. Here, Mrs. Cavendish describes her Near Death Experience.

O   O   O

MRS. CAVENDISH: They say the streets are paved with gold and the angels have wings. I was there. It ain't so. The strangest people were there to greet me. Mr. Cavendish took my hand and led me through a crowd of faces. Of course my mother and dad were there, but people I didn't really expect, too. My fifth grade teacher, Mrs. Peckham. I had an awful crush on her. The Quinn boy down the street, who used to deliver newspapers. I'd have him in for cookies and he would wrap his newspapers in plastic when it rained. And Abraham Lincoln, the greatest man that ever lived. Everyone who ever meant anything to me was there. They reached inside of me and embraced my heart. There was no man in white robes. No big booming voice. Just the feeling . . . the overpowering feeling of being loved. I'm going back. Someday I'm going back.

THE INNOCENTS' CRUSADE
by Keith Reddin

Helen, a postal worker, any age
Setting: a parking lot outside of a 6-plex, the present
Serio-Comic

*Helen here tells the frightening story of the day that one of her
co-workers ran amok with a gun.*

O   O   O

HELEN: I used to work for the postal system, and let me tell you,
working for the postal system for any length of time is enough
to make you lose all hope for Western Civilization.

I was working there every day, sorting mail, and one
morning Morty, he was fired two weeks earlier, he comes in,
he had a gun, it was a machine gun, he came in and he first
walks into the supervisor's office, he tells Mr. Wasserman to
get on the floor and then he shoots Mr. Wasserman in the
head, just like that, and then he goes down the hall and he
shoots Mr. Price, and then he shoots Thomas, and then he
points the machine gun at me and he says Hi, Helen, how are
you and I say oh not so great, Morty, why are you doing this,
why are you shooting people and he says because they fired
him and now he's gonna make everybody pay but then he
looks at me and says but not you, Helen, I'm not gonna shoot
you, and then he turns and blows Fred away, he puts this hole
in Fred's chest and I hear him going into the back and he
shoots Eric and Des and then he puts the gun in his mouth
and shoots himself and there's blood all over the place and
people are screaming and crying and I notice there's blood all
over me, I'm covered in blood, and I get up and I leave the
building and I don't ever come back, and I get to thinking why
didn't Morty shoot me, he shot all these other people but he
doesn't shoot me and I'm wondering what does it all mean,
nothing makes sense, and tonight was the first time I leave my
apartment in weeks and I go to this movie which was all about
people getting ripped apart and that upset me so I come out
to the parking lot and I hear Stephen talking to Laura and

some others and they're telling people to follow them and for the first time something starts to make sense and I'm thinking there might be a place for me and maybe we can do something and it started to seem right? You know? So . . . see you tomorrow. (*Helen exits.*)

IT IS IT IS NOT
by Manuel Periras García

Laura, a woman fearing desertion by her lover, 43
Setting: a beach house, the present
Serio-Comic

Laura fears that her lover of 20 years is about to leave her as she here confesses to Daniel, her lover's brother.

○   ○   ○

LAURA: I'm so glad you're here. I'm so glad. I couldn't have waited any more. It's been so long. And I have nobody. Nobody but you. Do you still love me. Can I trust you?

[**DANIEL:** (*Sitting on the floor.*) You can trust me but I can't keep a secret.]

LAURA: I can't trust you.

[**DANIEL:** Do you want comfort or secrecy?]

LAURA: I want her! She's leaving me! She's leaving me after all these years. After so many years! How can she do this to me? Has she told you?

[**DANIEL:** No.]

LAURA: She's leaving. She's left. She's never here. She's always out. The phone rings and she goes out. I don't answer the phone. It's never for me. It's always for her. Everybody calls her. She has friends. I have no one. I've left everyone for her and now she's leaving me. I've ceased to be myself for her and now she doesn't like me. She doesn't even like what I give her. On our anniversary I gave her flowers. A dozen red roses as I've given her for the past twenty years. We can no longer afford them still I made a sacrifice and bought them. She looked at them. Immediately I understood. She no longer cares. She doesn't care about me. She's leaving. I know. It is as if she has left already. Twenty years! We've been together twenty years. Do you want a drink?

[**DANIEL:** I'll have some coffee.]

LAURA: Coffee?!

[**DANIEL:** Yes.]

LAURA: (*Pouring another drink.*)

We don't have any coffee. Why should I buy coffee if we never have breakfast together anymore. She gets up in the morning and out she goes; has breakfast with who knows who. She just gets up and goes. She always slept late. She's always been slow. She's always taken hours to get dressed. Not anymore. She doesn't sleep late anymore. She gets up at seven and out she goes. By seven-o-five! She's out of here! Seven o'clock. Can you imagine that! Five minutes to get dressed. Can you imagine that! Diana. You know Diana. You've known her even longer than me. Has she ever! Ten in the morning used to be late for her. Not anymore. She doesn't even take a shower. And she's clean. She gets up. She gets dressed. And out she goes. In five minutes. She must take showers somewhere.

JANE AMPHETAMINE
by Annie G.

Jane, a young woman in dire straits, 20s
Setting: a bedroom, the present
Serio-Comic

Here, Jane makes a series of frantic phone calls in an effort to raise $250. She dials a number, obviously getting an answering machine.

O   O   O

JANE: Hi, Tony, this is Jane. I'm dressed like a muslim woman. Where are you? I haven't seen you in a week. I'll speak to you later. Bye.
(Hangs up and dials another number.)
Hi, Catharsis, this is Jane Amphetamine. I'm dressed like a Muslim woman. What are you doing? Moped tells me that you have a new job – dancing with the dummies in the windows at Bergdorfs, sounds like something you were born to do. Listen, I was wondering if you wanted to buy Mr. B. My cat. I know he was a stray, but I put at least $200 worth of shots in him – and I would sell him to you for $100. Oh, you hate my cat. What am I talking about I can't sell Mr. B to you, I love him. Could you lend me $200 then, it's kind of important, I can't tell you why. I paid you back. So what it wasn't in cash. That was a good turntable. So what no one uses turntables anymore. Okay, I'll see you in the window of Bergdorfs, bye.
(Hangs up and calls a number again.)
Hi, Tony, this is Jane again. I'm still dressed like a muslim woman. I had a dream last night. I was wondering if you wanted to hear it. Bye.
(Hangs up the phone. The phone rings.)
Hi, Mom, I'm dressed like a muslim woman. I'm glad you called, I'm having a crisis – yeah, I received the money for the drum set, yeah, I bought it – purple, with black trim around the base drum and black lettering of the band's logo – 2 white men in a kettle surrounded by cannibals. No, you can't see it

when you get to New York . . . No, I can not tell you why. Come on, ma, okay, I lost the drum set. Ma, stop yelling, I know it was your money, I know it was a birthday present, I already thanked you a thousand times. Ma, stop yelling, listen I'm having a crisis. Okay, okay, it was after a gig. I had a fight with Veronica and the witch wouldn't let me put my kit in her van – so I took a cab. I know I put my drum kit in the cab cause the driver was a pain in the ass and kept yelling at me with salami breath. I got home and I didn't have my drum set and that is all I know. I don't know where the set is, if I did then it wouldn't be lost. Ma, Ma, listen, Ma, okay, okay, don't you think I'm trying to be responsible. Ma, listen I really need your help. The lost drum set is the least of my worries. Well that's great, thanks for calling my life a catastrophe. Yeah, I'll see you next week when you come into New York.
(*Hangs up the phone.*)
Thanks for the fucking nurturance.
(*Dials a number – an answering machine again.*)
Hi, Tony, it's Jane, yeah I'm still dressed like a Muslim woman. I'm having a crisis and I need to talk to you. My number is 457-2897, in case you don't have your book with you. So I will speak to you later. Bye.
(*Starts drawing and playing the drums on a book and dancing to a song she is listening to. The phone rings.*)
Damn it, I lost the phone, follow the phone wire, follow the phone wire.
(*She finds it and answers.*)
Hi, Veronica, I'm dressed like a muslim woman. I was just talking about you. I have this great idea for this song, and you can sing the lead. When is the next band practice . . . What do you mean I can't practice if I don't have a drum set, I can borrow from someone. Well, don't you think I know that no one would want to lend me a drum set. But I'll find someone. Hold on I have another call. Candy! Guess what? No, I'm not dressed like a bumble bee, I'm dressed like a muslim woman. I'm on another call, I have to go. I made a collage for you. It's all about George Michael when he was fat. Could you lend me $65, no, speak to you later. Veronica, I'm back. Do you want to buy my leather jacket signed by Bono when he was hallucinating he was the reincarnation of Yoko Ono? I know it

would have been cooler five years ago, but it's still pretty cool. I'll sell it to you for $165. Do you think that I can borrow $150, it's really an emergency and I need the money. Yeah, I'll be at rehearsal.

(*Slams the phone down.*)

Bitch, she called me Sid and Nancy.

(*She starts taking off the "muslim woman outfit." Kicks some things out of the way.*)

Hi, Tony, it's Jane and I just want you to know that I'm *not* dressed like a Muslim woman. I am in a bind. I need $250 and I need it from you. I'm pregnant and it's your fault cause you had to have it in the goddamn phone booth and I think you're an asshole, and you weren't any good in bed anyway, and the only reason I started sleeping with you was cause you said you had an affair with Tina Turner. And I wonder if you have even enough balls to call me back, and even more balls to give me the goddamn money. Bye.

(*Slams the phone down.*)

Maybe I'll keep the baby.

JAY

by Anthony Giardina

Laurie, a young dancer, 20s
Setting: a train compartment, Penn Station, NYC
Serio-Comic

It can be extremely difficult to find fame and fortune in NYC, as Laurie here confesses to a stranger on a train.

O   O   O

LAURIE: I just left a guy.
(*Beat.*)
We were living together, I don't know, six months. That's over. I'm going home for awhile. I won't stay, don't get me wrong, I'll be back, right now I just can't stand the city.
[**JAY:** (*Beat.*) What happened?]
[**LAURIE:** What?]
[**JAY:** Between you and the guy?]
LAURIE: [Oh, that's personal. I don't have to tell you that.]
(*Beat.*)
He was cheatin' on me like crazy. Jesus, you know, like I don't mind once, twice, ya gotta expect that, but with him, it was like, what was I doing there?
(*Beat.*)
He was a dancer. That's what I am, too, a dancer. Well, no, I'm not. I don't know what the fuck I am. The city will do that to you, you know? It's like this occupational hazard. I came here, I wanted to be a dancer. I didn't have any training. I thought you could just *dance.* And the thing is, you know, this place is so nuts you can *do* that: you can just *dance.* The troupe I'm in, the Joyce McVeety Dance Company, we do like two, three gigs a year where we actually get paid. Rumsen Community College, they want a dance company and they can't afford anybody else, so they get us. And the rest of the year, we *train,* on account of Joyce is real serious and you never know when Rumsen is gonna call again. Does that make me a dancer?
(*She holds the question a second, then rejects it.*)

Anyway, that's where I met this guy and so now the whole thing is mixed up in my mind, like being a dancer and being with Joyce and being with him. Cause he slept with everybody else in the company and half the student body at Rumsen the last time we were there, so now there's a definite sleaziness attached to the whole business for me, not to mention various life-threatening diseases floating around. I feel like a Coke, you want a Coke?

JENNY'S NEW YEAR
by Annie G.

Jenny Glass, a young girl celebrating New Year's Eve with a
friend, 14
Setting: a den, New Year's Eve
Serio-Comic

*Jenny has holed up in her parents' den with some junk food and
a telephone. Here, she gabs with her best friend as the world
waits to welcome a new year.*

O   O   O

JENNY: Ten minutes to New Year's, are your parents at the
Goldberg's? Yea, so are mine. I think the whole neighborhood's there. Oh, Cathy, I wish you didn't have that stupid
pneumonia and were here with me now. Oh God, you can
hear the music. I know, it's so loud, it's like in my room
instead of being next door. Yea, Robin Meisner's party. You
know I wasn't invited. I knew I wouldn't be. If I was just 15
pounds lighter I'd be at that party. I just wish I could go to
sleep and all my fat would melt away and then I could fit into
those size 7 Guess jeans my mother bought 4 months ago.
But instead, I'm stuck wearing my brother's old Levis which fit
in the thighs but not in the waist, which is the only part of my
body I don't mind. But then I have to wear a belt and that
makes my tits look even more gigantic than they are, and they
are already too big. I wish they could just melt away too. Well,
at least you're lucky you don't have big tits. Oh, 8 minutes to
New Year's. Guess, guess, you know, come on, guess.
Malomars, they taste great, they're nice and stale. Oh God,
they're playing Vogue. What are you eating – Raisenettes,
Reeses Pieces, come on, tell me, oh, I know, Veal Cutlet
Parmigiana. Yes, how did I know? Our after school special.
Um, it tastes so good cold. Oh, it's frozen, how is it? I have to
try it. I bet Robin Meisner doesn't pig out like we do. I
overheard her once say she doesn't even eat birthday cake on
her birthday, and she loves cheese cake, but she can't afford
it! She's a stick. She is so skinny, there is not even one ounce

of fat on her. She was wearing this outfit today at school. She had this black leather mini-skirt, with these black fishnet stockings, a t-shirt that was really tight, these leopard boots with pointy toes and spikey heels and a really awesome faded denim jacket with the sleeves cut off, this big jewish star earring, her hair was sticking up all over the place, the brightest red lipstick, I swear she looked just like Madonna.

Cath, are you okay, that cough sounds really bad. You're my best friend ever. No one else will pig out with me like you do. Can you believe we went through one pound of Pistachio Nuts and a quart of Hagen Daz. I swear, it was a wet dream.

Oh, God, can you hear that, they're playing Prince, or symbol, whoever he is now. I'm so glad my parents went out, or else my mother would ask how come I wasn't invited to Robin's party, "you and Robin used to be best friends in the 5th grade." I don't think my mother has even noticed that I'm 14. I mean what could I say, look at me, I'm 20 pounds overweight – I don't get invited to those parties anymore. I wish she would understand something! Oh gosh, Cath, I don't think I told you, my parents really gave me shit last week cause when we went to New Jersey and the second we got over the bridge I just kissed the ground and gave thanks that I was privileged to be in the same state where Bruce was born and lived. My father was so pissed, cause I just opened the car door when we were still moving, and in line for the toll booth. Mother was pissed because she was afraid that someone she knew might be watching. Who do we know in New Jersey! Oh, but it was worth it, I swear the pavement almost smelled like him. My mother was so freaked out, she called the guidance counselor, Ms. Oracle, who's yours, same dummy. Great school system, this school sucks, not only did Ms. Oracle not know my name, but she kept calling me by the wrong one. She kept calling me Penny, and I kept saying Jenny, Jenny! So, I made up some story about how I thought I lost my good earrings . . . I told the guidance counselor that I didn't need any guidance, I just needed to lose 25 pounds and then everything would be okay. And she agreed with me!

Three minutes to New Year's. When is that pneumonia going to be done with, too bad my mother won't let me go visit you, she's so medicinal.

That song is still going . . .

(*She walks to the window.*)

Cath . . . I think I see Jake Pelman . . . He keeps stealing my pens. All day yesterday he kept shoving me into the lockers really hard. Then, right in front of everyone he tried to pick me up and shove me into my own locker and he said he was going to lock me up forever! It's a good thing I didn't fit, well being 17 pounds overweight does have some advantages, I guess. Do you think he likes me?

No, no you're not, no I'm fatter than you, you are not fatter than me. Okay, we're the same fatness. At least we're not the fattest ones in the ninth grade. Marcy Kaplan! She's fatter than everyone.

Well one minute to New Year's, and all I have left is the outside of these Oreos. Gee, maybe this will be a good year, and maybe this year I'll lose 25 pounds and then I'll be popular and have a boyfriend and then everything will be wonderful and my life will be perfect. And I'll bum all my fat clothes and we'll be really skinny for the rest of our lives, and never cheat on our diet again. Let's really go on a diet this year, Cath. Okay, tomorrow morning, definitely. But now it's New Year's and I've got these Oreos *and* 3 Milky Ways I hid for tonight. Well, if we're starting our diet tomorrow, I can eat as much as I want tonight, right?

Happy New Year, Cath!

JOHANNESBURG

by James Harrison

Johanna, the daughter of a fundamentalist, 17
Setting: a farm outside a small town in Ontario, 1939
Dramatic

Johanna is a young woman who longs to escape the dreary life she shares with her father. Here she confides an unhappy memory of her mother to a farm hand who she is encouraging to stand up to her father.

O   O   O

JOHANNA: Before my father started this church, we went to a bigger church, a Dutch Reform church. One day, my mother told him she wanted to leave. She wanted to go to a church where people weren't afraid of God. The elders of the church came to our house. There were eight men; they wore dark suits. I was twelve years old. I hid on the landing on the stairs and listened. These men, they said to my father, the church is the bride of Christ. They said my mother was committing adultery against Christ. They said the spirit of the devil had possessed her. As her husband in the eyes of God it was his duty, they said, to beat the devil out of her. When they left . . . he beat her. With his hands. He beat the spirit out of her, the bad spirits, the good spirits, everything . . . There are things God demands of us. God gave him a vision for this church. But that was after my mother died. She got sick after that. She just got sick and died.
(*He is asleep. She folds his arm down beside his head.*)
You have to keep your spirit.
(*She gently strokes his head and sings softly.*)
"On the third day Abraham lifted his eyes and saw the place far off."

JULIUS AND PORTIA JONES
by Brian Christopher Williams

Portia, a woman confronting her past, 30s
Setting: a nearly-deserted coal mining town, the present
Dramatic

As a child, Portia was sexually abused by her father, an ill-tempered coal miner. Years later, she returns home and finds him dying of Black Lung disease.

O   O   O

PORTIA: Don't you understand? Nothing is ever going to be alright. Nothing is ever going to change. I can't get away. I can't escape it. I was wrong when I said I don't take after anyone in this family, Pa. I take after you. You've taken any light I had in my soul and you've turned it dark and black and evil. And when someone comes along and opens the windows and lets in a little light you're right there to slam those shutters closed.

[**JOHN:** (*Big coughing fit.*)]

PORTIA: Die, old man. Die a slow and painful death. After you're gone, I'll be back. I'll make sure you don't get buried. I'll make sure the earth is not contaminated with your filth. I'll drag you down to the mine myself. I'll follow the smoke and I'll find the fire; someplace where the flame is so hot it melts the rocks into a flowing river, and I'll toss you in. And maybe, just maybe, when I'm sure your vile remains have been destroyed, maybe I'll do this world a service and I'll jump in after you.

KEELY AND DU
by Jane Martin

Keely, a pregnant woman taken hostage by a militant anti-
abortion group, 20-30
Setting: a basement in Rhode Island, the present
Dramatic

*Keely has been brutally raped by her ex-husband. While seeking
an abortion, she is kidnapped by members of an underground
anti-abortion group who intend to force her to carry the child to
term. Here, she longs for solitude.*

○   ○   ○

KEELY: I haven't ever been alone! Sharing with my brothers,
moving in with roommates, moving in with Cole, moving back
to Dad's, always other people in the room, always hearing
other people talk, other people cough, other people sleep.
Jesus! I dream about Antarctica, you know, no people, just
ice. Nobody on your side of the bed, no do this, don't do that,
no guys and what they want, what they have to have, just this
flat, white, right, as far, you know, as far as you could see, like
right out to the edge, no items, no chairs, no cars, no people,
and you can listen as hard as you want and you couldn't hear
one goddamn thing.

THE KING OF INFINITE SPACE
by *Andrew C. Ordover*

Julia, a woman living in a post-apocalyptic society, 20-30
Setting: a prison in a desert
Dramatic

Julia longs for love and beauty, but the world in which she lives is filled with hatred and pain. Here, she tells a story which mirrors her feelings.

O   O   O

JULIA: There's a story they told us at the school:
(*Chorus provides music and rhythm.*)

On a plain and arid field
In the middle of a nothing
A sapling poked out of the ground
Without invitation or reason
He said:
All around is flat and brown
But all above is majesty blue
I will grow tall and wide
To reach the blue
The blue which turns to black at night
Glittering with a billion sparkling stars
And I will live among the stars

Years passed and he grew
Tall and wide, as he had promised
And other trees poked out
To join him in his quest

Now the tree is old
If you ask him about the stars
He will shake his head sadly
And tug at the roots which hold him
"I will never live among the stars"
He says

"I must always live among the trees
The many trees . . ."

And I . . . I . . .
I am in a forest too
Surrounded by majestic trees
Protected by their branches
And shaded by their leaves
They have made an arid plain better
They give comfort to a difficult land

What comfort, I wonder
Do they find in each other
Or are their eyes
Even still
On the stars?

LIGHT SENSITIVE
by Jim Geoghan

Edna, a woman fighting for the man she loves, 30s
Setting: an apartment in Hell's Kitchen, the present
Dramatic

Edna has fallen in love with Tom, a blind man to whom she has volunteered to read. When Tom's best friend arrives on the scene, Edna fears that he will waste no time in supplying Tom with an unflattering description of her. Here, she begs him to remain silent.

○   ○   ○

EDNA: When we fall in love with someone there's a moment when we take a picture of that person, an emotional snapshot, that we carry with us forever. If we're lucky, if we're very, very lucky, the person we fall in love with will always resemble that snapshot.

[**LOU:** What are you talking about?]

EDNA: I'm talking about loving someone. Thomas is getting ready to fall in love with me. He hasn't felt like he's worth doing that in a very long time but his self respect is . . . well, you saw him. He's different now. Thomas is changing. We'll be in Times Square tonight. We'll both be drinking. He'll kiss me at midnight and sketch a picture in his mind that will last him a lifetime. Nothing will change it. Not even if you wait a day to tell him what you think is so important. I've never been surer of anything. When my father met my mother it was the height of the Depression and no one had very much of anything. But my father had just had his twentieth birthday and an uncle from somewhere had sent him a five dollar bill. In 1939, five dollars was big money.

[**LOU:** Look . . .]

EDNA: No! You're going to listen! If you're going to take Thomas from me then the least you can do is listen!

(Calms herself – then.)

My father asked my mother out. It was the middle of July. He took her to Coney Island. I think she was impressed with that.

Other boys took my mother to the theater or concerts but my father chose a place that catered to pleasing all five of the senses and it sparked something in her that night. They rode the carousel six times in a row. You were supposed to exit the carousel at the end of each ride and get back on line but my father wouldn't budge and the man running the carousel wasn't about to challenge him. Besides, they were sitting on the bench and demand for the bench was low. My father listened to every word my mother said that night as though she were the most intelligent, fascinating woman he had ever met. More than that he thought she was funny. Yes. She made him laugh. It made her feel very special. To make a person feel they are bright is one thing. But to make them feel they are witty and clever . . . They went on some other rides, the Ferris wheel, I believe, the wild mouse . . . My father bought my mother a bag of peanuts. He tipped the man selling them an extra nickel and she thought he was "devilishly mad." Then my mother didn't feel too well, probably one of the rides. They sat on a bench on the boardwalk. By now it was much cooler and my father put his jacket around her. They spent the rest of their night sitting on that bench talking. My mother has shown me the bench. I've *seen* "the bench." The lights danced behind them, music blared from one of the rides, there was the unmistakable smell of hot dogs and cotton candy. And in the middle of all that, when the moment was absolutely right, my mother took her snapshot of my father. She fell in love and this was the man and the moment she would remember until the day she dies. She tucked away her photo in her soul. Some years after that night, my father ceased to find my mother funny. He also did not find her interesting or intelligent or any of the other things he found her to be that night. I have watched my father conduct a campaign of disinterest and of no love for my mother that few men can equal. All I can do is pray there is a God for if there is He will surely send my father to Hell for what he has wasted. Was it last week or the week before . . .? I'm not sure but my father was on his way out and my mother, what's *left* of my mother, came shuffling by and she looked at my father only out of the corner of her eye because full eye contact ended years ago, and my father was just putting on his scarf and tossed it over his shoulder and I suppose, for the briefest moment, he resembled something called dashing to someone like my mother who still listens to big band music, and at that very same moment he decided to take some pity on his lifelong victim and so he said to my mother, "Adios, sweetie!" and the old woman's eyes filled with colored lights and cotton candy! You could almost hear a calliope playing in the background. Her face! Her expression! The life that flared up in her! "There! That's him! The kind and gentle man who loves me!" She forgave *everything*! He was the handsome young man on the bench again. It was only for a second but a second was all it took. It made my mother's day! It made her *life*! When father came home later and resumed his ritualistic abuse she was able to take her daily quota of humiliation *beautifully*! After all – that wasn't the real him. She had seen the *real* him earlier that day. I could love Tom from a place like that! Only he would never betray me. He would be too busy being glad he was loved. I would make Tom so happy. You saw him! Running out to buy champagne . . . wearing his favorite Christmas sweater! The one he thinks is red and green! He stood by the sink and recited a poem for me! A poem he memorized in high school! What am I going to do with the picture I took of him? What will I do with my picture?!

THE LINE THAT PICKED UP 1000 BABES
(And How It Can Work For You)
by Eric Berlin

Fran, a woman dragged to a singles bar by her friend, 20-30
Setting: a singles bar
Serio-Comic

*When Fran meets an interesting man in a bar, she tells him of
her frustration with "guys."*

○   ○   ○

FRAN: I only came here one other time. That was enough. I went
up to the bar to get a drink and this guy came over to me and
he said – (*Mimics his superior, flirtatious tone.*) "*HI*!" in this
way that implied what he was really saying was, "Boy, are *you*
lucky. Of all the girls here, I've decided to talk to *you*!" Lucky
me. He said to me, "What''s your name?" I said, "Fran." He
said, "That's a beautiful name." Fran? Fran. The name my
father gave me out of revenge when I wasn't born a boy. Fran
is a lot of things but none of them is beautiful. No. So, then
he says, "Hey! You Italian?" I said, "No," and start to walk
away, but he *grabs my arm* and says "Hey! You Irish?" "What
is this? NO! Goodbye!" And he says, "So! What are you
then?" "Nothing! I'm nothing!" I said. And he stopped, and
he looked at me, and he said, "Oh. I guess you're right.
You're nothing." And he smiled this *smile* at me that really
made him king of the mountain. This *smile* that said that I was
nothing because I wouldn't talk to him, this *GUY*. Men are
bad enough, but there's nothing worse than *GUYS*. He called
me nothing. This asshole with the top two buttons of his shirt
open to show that he had *no* chest hair. This *guy* with his
conceited, judgmental smile. Called me "nothing." Should
that have bothered me? What he thought? Maybe not. But it
did. So I left. If this is where this guy belongs, then it's not
where I belong, so I left. And never came back 'til Ellen
dragged me here tonight. And since then, I have this bias
against guys I meet in bars. Maybe I shouldn't, but I do, there
it is.

LION IN THE STREET
by Judith Thompson

Joanne, a woman dying of cancer, 30s
Setting: a restaurant
Serio-Comic

When Joanne finds out that she has terminal bone cancer, she tells her best friend how she would like to die.

O   O   O

JOANNE: Ya know, I have to go to the bathroom, like, real bad but I'm not gonna go, ya know why? Cause every time . . . I sit down to pee I feel my whole life drainin' out of me, just draining out with the pee, goin' . . . outa me, into the water down in the pipes, and under the . . . friggin' . . . GROUND. That's where I'll be, Rho, that's where I'm gonna . . . (*Fights to retain her composure.*) I'll come home with the groceries? Like after dark? and I'll see Frank and the kids through the window, in the livin'-room, right? Watchin' TV, or drawing on paper, cuttin' out stuff, whatever, and I'll stand on the porch and watch 'em, just . . . playing . . . on the floor, and I think . . . that's life, that's life goin' on without me, it'll be just like that, only I won't be here with the groceries, I'll be under the ground under the ground with my flesh fallin' off a my face and I just can't take it.

LOOSE KNIT
by Theresa Rebeck

Margie, scattered and erratic; always at the end of her rope, 30s
Setting: a sushi restaurant, the present
Serio-Comic

*When Margie goes out on a blind date with Miles, an anal
retentive perfectionist, she cracks under his intense scrutiny.*

        O   O   O

MARGIE: You have a very nice car!

[**MILES:** Thank you.]

MARGIE: I've never actually seen a Silver Shadow before. I mean,
it's so, you know, decadent, it's great.

[**MILES:** Decadent.]

MARGIE: I don't mean decadent, I mean, decadent in a good
way. I mean, you know, decadent, excessive, wasteful – no,
that's not what I mean. I don't know what I mean. Forget I
said it.

[**MILES:** (*Cold.*) I do think it's important to have beautiful
things in your life. Is that what you mean?]

MARGIE: [Yes! That's what I mean!] I mean, it's great to have
beautiful things in your life and while that might seem kind of
decadent to a lot of people, it's not, really, because unless you
have too much money, which is not really possible, because
then you can have, like, beautiful things. You know what I
mean. (*Pause.*) Don't you?

[**MILES:** No. (*He writes.*)]

MARGIE: (*Abashed.*) Well. I do think it's nice to have beautiful
things. In your life. I wish I had beautiful things in my life. I
wish I had your car in my life. I mean, I'm glad it's in my life.
It's in my life tonight, anyway, and I find that really just –
wonderful. And I find you fascinating, but I also; want to tell
you to fuck off. Do you know what I mean? I mean, I don't
really want to tell you to fuck off, really what I want to do is
have sex in the back seat of that amazing car, but frankly, I
don't know, I'm really just so stunned by all this, stunned and
repulsed, you know? The thought of kissing you makes my

53

blood run cold but on the other hand, I'm really hoping that you'll pick me. Pick me, Miles. Pick me. Let's not waste time. That's why I signed up for that stupid dating service, because I didn't want to waste any more time, I don't have any more time to waste, but women aren't supposed to do that sort of thing, we don't choose, do we, you guys are the ones who do the choosing. Well, sometimes we FORGET THAT, ALL RIGHT? I wish I would shut up; I really do but I just don't think that's going to happen. What is the matter with me? Why can't I do this? I'm really sorry. It's just, you know – you can't just be like this, but you are, and I – I want you. I want to fuck you in the back seat of that car. You make me sick.

LOOSE KNIT

by Theresa Rebeck

Gina, a no-nonsense attorney, 30s
Setting: an apartment in Manhattan, the present
Serio-Comic

*When Gina is let go from her law firm, her usual reserve begins
to crack a bit.*

○   ○   ○

GINA: Oh, no. I didn't get fired. I was let go. They let me go. Like
a balloon.
(*She hands drinks out. They all watch her.*)
[**LIZ:** When did . . .]
GINA: IT DOESN'T MATTER. (*Pause.*) I don't care. We're
streamlining the department, see, and that's just that. I put my
time in, eighty hour weeks, I work hard, my research is better
than anybody's, and I'm the only person in the entire building
who knows how to run the computers. And it doesn't matter.
They don't care. You want to know why the city is falling
apart? Because they fire everybody who knows what they're
doing. It's policy. If you know what you're doing, you get
fired.
[**LIZ:** But don't they have to . . .]
GINA: They don't have to do anything. They only have to do what
they want. And Morrison doesn't like me because I'm a
woman. It's also because I know what I'm doing, but she'd be
able to handle that if I weren't a girl. She's one of *those*
women, you know, one of the ones who only likes men?
What am I talking about; we're all the same. You're all, the
first thing you think is that I screwed up somehow, that's the
way the logic works. Women are the worst, and that's the
truth. We're always watching each other like sharks; they
don't have to do it to us anymore because we're only too
willing to do it to ourselves. And who comes into the picture
but little Mr. Harvard Law. The kid's killing time! Everybody
knows it. In six months he's going to land a spot with
Debuvois and Plimpton, whatever, he's out of here, he's doing

his public service time so he can have a nice little mark on his CV. We're a SLOT on his RESUMÈ and she thinks he's God's gift. I don't care. If I were black, you can bet it would be different. I'm sorry for being a racist, Paula, no one wants to be a racist but these morons making the decisions don't leave you any choice! Davenport stays because he's black, and Mr. Harvard Law stays because he's Mr. Harvard Law, and I go because I'm a single white woman in my thirties and it doesn't mean shit what I do. Let's face it. We're the most useless group of people history has ever heard of; we're a bunch of fucking spinsters, that's what we are. I wish I was married. I wish I was black. Or no, you know what I wish? I wish everybody who got in – you know, everybody who got *in* – would turn into white men. All of them. Those Asian women newscasters, and those sleazy black male weather guys, all those snappy little white girls who look great in power suits – I wish they would just turn into white men over fifty. I wish all of them would turn into Bill Buckley. Because then we would *know*. We would know who the good guys were, and who the bad guys were. We would just know who was who and what was what.

(*She starts to unravel her knitting.*)

But it's fine, okay? Everything is fine. If this were, you know, India or something, *Iran,* maybe then I'd be in trouble. Not only would I be out of a job, I'd have to wear one of those stupid black things over my face. Right? But this is America. It's better here than anywhere in the world. Everything is fine.

THE MIDNIGHT MOONLIGHT
WEDDING CHAPEL
by Eric Berlin

Misty, a woman looking for love, 20-30
Setting: a wedding chapel in Las Vegas
Serio-Comic

Misty and Peter have decided to get married after only just meeting in a Las Vegas casino. Here, Misty tells the justice of the peace of the events that led to their hasty decision.

O   O   O

MISTY: I never do anything.
   [**MARIE:** What?]
MISTY: I mean, I *eat* and stuff. Like Peter says he still has fun sometimes, but, I mean . . . Like, I play slot machines – ten dollars out of every paycheck. No more. And I don't put my winnings back in again, either, I keep them. That's how the casinos make their money, you know, from people winning money and giving their money right back. So I do that and I waitress at the Tropicana. And guys try to pick me up, and sometimes I go out with other waitresses, but that's, like, what we go out and do is pretty much the same as *our jobs.* I mean, I thought Vegas was going to be really exciting when I first moved here, to be a dancer, but it really isn't, you know? So I really don't do much. Waitress. Audition. Do the slots. Slots are all I really like because it's all fate, just you and the machine, right? I can always feel which slot machine is going to pay off. It's like I always know which way to go. That's how I met Peter, I told him which machine to play, and he did and he won all that money, so we got drunk and then we decided to do this. This is the most fun I've had in a long time. Thank you for not closing! I mean that.

NORTHEAST LOCAL
by Tom Donaghy

Gi, a new mother, 20s
Setting: the home of Mickey and Gi
Dramatic

Gi welcomes her baby son home with the following speech.

○   ○   ○

GI: Gonna be beautiful. Gonna be strong and things will happen
to you. You know, special things like events or something.
Cause things will happen cause you're better than most.
Putting a spell on you to be better than most. Poof. That's a
spell word, magicians go "poof." And the spell is so's your . . .
nose will be much nicer than mine. And so's . . . you'll have
Mick's legs. That's the green-eyed man who was just here,
giving me grief. He puts pieces a steel together. And he's your
father.

Gotta know that at some point. And, uh, the more spell is
you won't ever have acne ever . . . and I'll have beautiful,
black hair without any silver in it till you're a famous old man
who has to give lectures in Paris, France and then looks good
with silver hair so it'll be something you'll want to have. And
at these lectures you're giving you'll be communicating with
all different types of people cause the world will be better by
then and they'll all be in the audience asking you about your
mother and you'll go, yes, she was a great woman and a
famous artist but I am much more famous than her cause
there's a spell on me and besides the best and only thing
about her is she always had the most beautiful, black hair that
was nothing like the silver hair I now have on my head as I
stand here at the podium. (*She cries.*) Just crying all the time
now for no reason and it's the worst thing when you've got
really nothing to cry about to be bawling like a baby. Cause if
you start the baby bawling it's all over. (*Pause.*) Mick planted
another rhododendron which means it's you, so you'll see it
when you're older. (*She looks down at the child.*) You'll see
many things your whole life, cause I put a spell on you . . .
Stephan Carey Michael. (*Kisses baby.*)

AN OLD ACTRESS IN THE ROLE OF DOSTOEVSKY'S WIFE
by Edvard Rodzinsky

An Old Actress, a woman remembering her past, 70s
Setting: an old age home in Russia
Serio-Comic

Here, an old actress remembers her first kiss and her first love.

O   O   O

AN OLD ACTRESS: He was always there! As long as I can remember, I would fall asleep at night imagining him. During the day I would see him, like Pushkin's Hermann, standing outside the window waiting, and waiting . . . I hated all my domestic comfort. I wanted the unknown . . . the darkness in which . . . he was hidden! And then late one evening . . . I opened the door – and slipped out into the spring night. I walked about the dark city . . . a breathless young girl, tasting freedom and fear! And I knew, I knew that I would see him! . . . Suddenly I felt a hand on my shoulder! He pulled me into a waiting droshky . . . Heavens, there were still droshkys then! The horses raced, he turned up my face and suddenly in horror I saw his idiotic moustache . . . and something old and frightening . . . He kissed me . . . and I, as in a dream, looked over his shoulder . . . And I saw my window . . . we were passing right by my house . . . The light was burning there . . . And I remembered my favorite lamp, my father's footsteps . . . With a scream, I jumped out . . . I came to in my own bed . . . in the bliss of illness . . . I had a fever . . . To this day, I don't know whether all that happened . . . or whether it was just a young girl's feverish dream . . .

THE OLD LADY'S GUIDE TO SURVIVAL
by Mayo Simon

Netty, an Old Lady, 70-80
Setting: a bus stop, San Diego, the present
Serio-Comic

Netty's eyes are failing, and here she complains about eye doctors as she tries to catch a bus. Normally she's a vigorous old lady, always in control of her life. But something has happened to her eyes. As she comes across the stage, traffic noise is heard, then angry horns.

O   O   O

NETTY: *(Shouting at the horns.)*
All right, all right, have a heart! Give me a chance!
(She continues hesitantly until she reaches a bench, which she grabs with relief.)
Oooh!
(She laughs, takes a deep breath, sits.)
Now I can wait for the bus.
(She turns slightly and squints out of the corner of her eye.)
And from here I can also check on my bank without them seeing me. My account is across the street with the Security Pacific, formerly Union Bank. They're not too strong. I heard on Money Line last night five more banks in trouble. Two in New York. *Three* in California. I called the Security Pacific, formerly Union Bank. They said the bank is strong. But *I heard* you closed down your foreign operations. Well, they said, we're just sticking to what we do best. I don't know. I'm watching this very carefully.
(Notices something.)
Ah! The bank is opening. I'm watching.
(She leans sideways, squinting.)
I want to make sure nobody's running in. That could mean panic.
(Continues watching.)
They say I can't see. But I see what I have to.
(Satisfied there is no bank panic this morning, Netty

continues.)

I'll tell you something. A year ago – six months ago – I had excellent vision. Better than excellent. Outstanding. Then one morning I get up, I look in the mirror, I can't see myself. I look all around in the mirror, I'm not there. Instead of my face, a black splotch. They say when you get old you become invisible to the world. But not to yourself, God forbid.

(Netty hears something.)

The bus?

(Tries to look up the street.)

. . . No.

(Continuing the story.)

So immediately I go for a check-up. I say, Doctor Bronstein, I'm not clicking on all cylinders. I can't see myself in the mirror. I feel like I'm disappearing. Well, he says, it could be cataracts. Or it could be the macular degeneration. *If* it's cataracts, there's a wonderful operation. So he sends me to another doctor. An oph-thal-molo-gist. The first of many.

(Hears something.)

There it is.

(A bus is heard approaching, Netty squints.)

Can't make out the number.

(Yelling, waving.)

Number Five? Number Five?

(The bus passes with a roar.)

See? Invisible.

(Pause.)

Maybe it was out of service.

(She squints at the other empty bench.)

If there was only another person here. I could get a drop of help.

(Shrugs, returns to the story.)

All right: The first oph-thal-molo-gist. I won't mention his name. I don't want any trouble. Let's just say he wasn't for me. It's not necessary to go into all the gory details.

(She drums her fingers on the bench until she can restrain herself no longer.)

His girl, who can't be more than eighteen years old, calls me Netty. All right, *Netty*, she says. I said, I prefer Mrs. Greene. She, from the Queens Garden, doesn't like that. All right, *Mrs.*

Greene, she says, with that little touch of sarcasm which I hate. I say nothing. I know how to speak up, you can believe me. But I'm here to see the doctor.

(*Netty sighs.*)

He doesn't greet me. *He* doesn't waste words. Gives me a very thorough examination –

(*Netty bangs her head on the bench as she delivers the doctor's verdict.*)

Cataracts! He does the operation in the hospital, I go home the same day. I try to tell him my other symptoms. All day long the sun is so penetratingly bright on my eyes, I can't bear it, and at night I see sparkling lights and dark whirling comets, like a – like a Van Gogh picture. But he's not interested.

(*Shakes her head.*)

I call Doctor Bronstein and tell him he sent me to a very fine doctor, but I'd like a second opinion. Who does he recommend? The second doctor, Doctor Conners –

(*With approval.*)

– an older man – gives me a superb examination. I tell him all my symptoms. He listens with great sympathy, great understanding. He too says cataracts. But it could be something more. There may be bleeding behind the retina. That could mean the macular degeneration. He can operate, but if it's the macular degeneration, it won't help and could even hurt. And if he doesn't operate? "Then you'll be blind."

(*Shprintzy, another old lady, has walked up leaning on a clawed support cane. She's small and bird-like, with ribbons in her straw-colored hair. She sits down on the other bench, as Netty continues.*)

Can I tell you how that word affected me? For five years since my husband Jack died I've lived alone. Everything on my own. I go myself to the university. I study at the ICL, the Institute for Continued Learning, where I'm naturally the oldest in every class. I write, I shop, I cook. I do all my household work. I invest my money as best I can. I keep up with the news. I go to plays and concerts. I plan trips. I love to plan trips. And once in a while I even take one.

(*Laughs.*)

I'm planning now for Alaska. It's supposed to be a gorgeous trip. And it will most likely be my last trip. But . . . blind?

(*Pause.*)

A week ago at the bus stop, I meet a woman. Young. Beautiful. And she had the *same problem* with her eyes. *And* she was just coming from her doctor. She had the operation. Her eyes – *perfect*. It's like a miracle. No, not *like* a miracle, she says. It *is* a miracle. He's the miracle doctor. I have to see him. All right, I'll make an appointment. Where is he? You know San Diego is an enormous city. If you have to travel everywhere by bus, it can be very hard. I can't read the street signs anymore, and I can't see pot holes. I try not to be, but sometimes I get a little anxious about falling. I'm not afraid. I'm never afraid . . . But if I should fall . . .

(*Netty completes the thought with a gesture. A bus is heard coming.*)

The bus!

(*She jumps up.*)

This one's not getting away from me.

RAFT OF THE MEDUSA
by Joe Pintauro

Cora, an HIV-positive woman, 20-30
Setting: a group therapy session
Dramatic

Here, Cora breaks down at her AIDS support group and finally explains how she became infected.

O   O   O

CORA: Felicia, for whatever it's worth . . . (*Sighs.*) There's a restaurant called Docks under the building where I worked. Big seafood place with a singles bar, forty percent women, sixty percent men; the majority of which are married men on the make. I'd say thirty-five percent of the men are single, five percent are straight-looking gays who come to put the make on the fifteen percent of the male population that can be had: In other words, a normal bar. I ate dinner there one night and noticed there's some fifty spotlights far up, it's a high ceiling – and under one of those spotlights I noticed this woman. She was a standout, really, white collar, dark, super-silky chestnut hair. You couldn't tell if she was beautiful or not but the way the light fell on her made everyone else look pretty dingy. All the men noticed her. I measured her position under the spotlight – five spindles down on the brass rail where it curves, and I said to myself, Christmas is a couple days away I'm tired of being depressed and alone and I said, hell, I'm giving myself the best shampoo, conditioner and *rinse* and I'm coming back to this place to stand at that fifth spindle under that spotlight. I am not the low esteem type that desires to be a dick cushion for any horny executive, O.K.? I just wanted to be out there in the predator's market. I wanted to be . . . bidded for, desired; to test my power to attract, I mean there is some satisfaction even for a normal woman to occasionally need to test her – (*Cutting herself off.*) Well, O.K. The guy who started talking to me was like an Irish peasant – red cheeks, smooth skin, grey suit, red tie – but there was a waft of something nice and Catholic that crossed these real blue eyes. Really nice teeth. He

64

was cute. We both had roommates. So we went to the Best Western Motor Lodge on the West Side, you know the one, with the big yellow sign, and it was not as boring as I'd expected mainly because he was intelligent, interesting – and we made a date and did it again, *and* again and uh, I thought . . . if I wanted to . . . I could fall in love with this guy. Well, he was gay. I mean bi. This I never suspected. He sprang it on *me* when I sprang it on *him* that I really liked him. He abruptly ended it. I said, "so, it was fear of intimacy," that he was using the gayness as an excuse not to hurt me . . . I wasn't his type, so, I forgot about it. That was 1986. He stopped answering my calls. Immediately after, I met my . . . now husband, another Catholic, a lawyer, and . . . uh, a year ago I started with thrush and tiredness and a horrible . . . um, a terrible rash. We took the test. I was positive, my husband was negative. I confessed to him about the guy and he insisted we track him down. Leonard . . . Leonard Kelleher was his name and he was dead of AIDS. I have the virus.

REDWOOD CURTAIN
by Lanford Wilson

Geri, an Asian-American musical prodigy, 17
Setting: Geneva's home in Arcata, Calif., the present
Dramatic

The daughter of a Vietnamese woman and an American GI, Geri is obsessed with finding her father. Here, she tells her Aunt Geneva why she can no longer handle the pressure of being a concert pianist.

○   ○   ○

GERI: I'm not tired, damnit, I've just had it. And I don't think it's at all unusual or sick or egocentric to want to be a normal human being or to be liked or appreciated in something.

[**GENEVA:** You're appreciated. Enormously.]

GERI: I'm not appreciated, I'm "special." Every time I walk out onstage. "Oh, isn't she tiny, isn't she just adorable. She's a Vietnam War bastard, you know. She has no idea who her mother and father are. Aren't we lucky one of them turned out to be special." Sony Classical wanted to call my album "America's Children"!

And I don't see why having a talent or a gift, even if it's for just sticking at something and sitting on my rear end and practicing, which is all I have, anyway – I have a tolerance for repeating scales and exercises ad nauseam; apparently I enjoy my fingers swelling up and having my nails bleed and walking around with Band-Aids on all my fingers – and I don't know why someone with whatever that is, that gift or curse or liability or handicap (it's like you can only be given something, even of whatever questionable value, if you're simultaneously eviscerated of everything anyone holds as worthy or admirable or real or worthwhile), I don't know why someone like that has to be treated like a freak of nature, like they have seven arms like Shiva or however many he has, and tiptoed around like they're sick or maimed or consumptive or an invalid or special in some way. I don't want to be special.

SCREWED-UP WOMEN AND
THE MEN BEHIND THEM
by Barbara Sellars

Francine, a promiscuous New Yorker, 20-30
Setting: a quilting bee for the Names Quilt Project, the present
Serio-Comic

Francine prowls the meat markets every night in search of sex with strangers. Here, she tells the tale of an encounter that didn't turn out quite the way she planned.

○   ○   ○

FRANCINE: I had sex with a stranger last night. I don't want to brag, but usually it's easy for me to pick up a guy in a bar. This was at a drugstore. I was picking up some Advil before I headed out for the evening, and the guy on line right in front of me was getting some condoms from the cashier. Extra-large condoms. And this guy was taking his time and being very picky. I watched the whole thing like I was at the movies. First, he examined the Trojan extra-large, read the label, checked the price, read the label again. Then he looked at Erotica extra-large, then Excita, then He-Man, and Super He-Man. And he kept pointing to the ones he wanted to look at, saying, "No, not those. Those. The extra-large. Extra-large." Meanwhile, the line behind me was getting longer and longer and everybody was captivated. Finally he found what he wanted, but when he took his wallet out he didn't have enough money. So, of course, I offered to pay the balance, it was only a couple of bucks. Listen, I saw my chance, and I grabbed it. I wanted to see that condom on. So we're walking down the block together towards my apartment. And then we're sitting on my couch, just talking and he seems perfectly fine to just talk, so I'm about to make the first move myself, what else is new, when he bursts into tears and starts sobbing on my shoulder. He tells me he's gay! The condoms were for his lover, his own penis was really quite small, it's always been an issue for him. They needed two sets of condoms, extra-large and extra-small, and his lover would always make him

67

buy both pairs at the same time just to confuse the people at the store for fun, but he wouldn't do it. He'd buy the large ones at Love's, then go down the block and buy the small ones at Rite-Aid. And it was beginning to get to him. So, I offered him some wine and we talked some more. He was so nice. I told him he should drop this guy and look for somebody smaller. Then we traded phone numbers and planned to do brunch. And then I went back out, went to my favorite bar, and had sex with someone else.

SERPENT IN THE NIGHT SKY
by Dianne Warren

Joy, a teenaged runaway, 17
Setting: a small town stretching along the shore of an immense
lake in Northern Saskatchewan, the present
Dramatic

*Joy has hitched a ride to Saskatchewan with Duff, whom she
now intends to marry. Following an argument, Joy tells Duff of
the loneliness that she has experienced since leaving home.*

○   ○   ○

JOY: You know, before you came along, I was scared. I was
standing by the side of the road and it was getting dark and I
was scared. Then you stopped and you were grinning and you
had on that brand new cowboy hat. You reminded me of
somebody's brother. No one in particular. Just somebody's
brother. You gave me a lift and we . . . we spent the night in
that motel. (*Pause.*) After you went to sleep I lay there as close
as I could get to the edge of the bed. The sheets were
touching me all over, cold and starchy, and I was afraid to
move. I lay like that for a couple of hours, then you woke up.
You moved over close to me, so we were both on the edge of
the bed, and you put your arm over me and moved your head
into my neck. And you were warm. You were so . . . warm.
And I felt myself putting my arms around you and you held
onto me and I held onto you and it was . . . it was like we
were going to fall . . . just fall through space forever if we
didn't hold on. (*Pause.*) Now I'm afraid again. I'm afraid if I
leave I'll just start falling through space.

SINGLE AND PROUD
by Frederick Stroppel

Jackie, an associate professor teaching a seminar on dating and
sex appeal, 40s
Setting: a dating seminar, the present
Serio-Comic

*Jackie's seminar is entitled: "Power Dating for the 90s: A Guide
for Savvy Singles." Somewhere behind her psycho-babble
rhetoric lurks an abhorrence for the opposite sex, as may be seen
in the following speech.*

O   O   O

JACKIE: It's just as you said, Jeanette: they're all the same. All cut
from the same worthless cloth. I have stacks and stacks of
research that will bear this out. The average male by the age
of forty will have slept with twenty-two point six women,
betrayed one point eight wives, seduced three point four
female employees, and fondled ninety-eight separate breasts.
This hound-like behavior is inborn in the species – it would
take decades of genetic engineering to weed out the deficient
strain. So many times I've felt a twinge of regret after this
class, knowing that the single woman I was sending out into
the world filled with enthusiasm and optimistic cant was
destined to fall victim to the devious lust and manipulative
malevolence of her brutish male counterpart – all my positive
lessons and happy thoughts trampled in his Neanderthal
wake. If I weren't such an "up" person, I'd be almost bitter.
So don't waste your sympathy, honey. If he hasn't screwed
you personally, you can bet that he's screwed someone just
like you, or he will in the near future. They can't help it, the
poor misguided beasts. They just can't be civilized. Does that
clear it up for you?

SNAKEBIT

by David Marshall Grant

Jennifer, an actress-turned-baker, 30-40
Setting: a house in L.A., the present
Serio-Comic

Here, Jennifer tells her best friend why she hates acting.

O   O   O

JENNIFER: I don't want to be an actress. I hate acting. I've always hated acting. It fills me with nothing but self-loathing. There, I said it. And you know, even if I somehow got a part, and somehow didn't get fired, which could easily happen, considering all the producers are openly weeping that they never managed to get somebody famous in this horrible part that I somehow miraculously got, then I get to have some evil critic project all his self-loathing and personally attack me with such wry, snappy humor, everybody in New York laughs about it. And that doesn't matter really. You do your affirmations, you know, your prayers that you'll be like, you know, so filled with self-love, that all that won't matter . . . What am I saying? The whole thing's a joke. You know why I don't want to act? And don't tell Jonathan this, I've never told anybody this. I started to stutter. Can you believe that? Honestly. I would pick a word in the script, and when I came to it, I wouldn't be able to say it. I would freeze. I couldn't get it out.
[**MICHAEL:** You started to stutter.]

JENNIFER: On stage. Or when I had to read from something. What do you think that means? It's sad, isn't it? It's pathetic.

SPINE

by Bill C. Davis

Claire, 13, talking to her dying brother, 11
Setting: a country home in Connecticut, the present
Dramatic

Claire's younger brother, Christy, is dying. Here, she speaks to him for what she knows will be the last time.

○   ○   ○

CLAIRE: It's really weird that you can't talk. But I know what you want to say. I do. You want to say, "Claire – you're a very good sister." And I want to say, "You're a very good brother " – you are, Christy. You're a better brother than Mike. I guess that's not saying very much. Charlene and Reesy and Jenny ask about you. They worry about you. They worry that you're having pain, cause I told them when I've heard you yell. I didn't tell them when you cried – I wouldn't do that. But a few times you screamed. The first time you did that, I was so scared. It was the most scared I've ever been until just a little while ago – until just before I gave you your present. That was the most scared I've ever been. But that's not my secret. (*Pause.*) I thought something awful once – not too long ago. Remember July fourth? You wanted us to go to the lake and I wanted us to go to the ocean, because they have the best fireworks; in the sky and in the water – like stereo. But you wanted to go fishing in the lake. I was real mad, was so mad, because that's what always happens. Whenever you want to go somewhere that's where we always go. And I wished something awful – I was wrong – I know I was, but I wished … I said to myself, "I wish he'd hurry up and …" (*She can't say it.*) It was bad to think that, and I really didn't think it long. I just wanted to see the fireworks from the boats. and that's not what I wish. I wish you'd never die. That's what I really wish, Christy. I'm sorry. Blink that you forgive me. (*Christy blinks.*)
Thanks Christy. (*Claire kisses him. She leaves his bed and goes to Lois.*) Mom. . . .

STANTON'S GARAGE

by Joan Ackerman

Mary Louise, an earthy woman helping out in her friend's garage, 60
Setting: a small service station in upstate Missouri, the present
Serio-Comic

While she makes egg salad, Mary Louise entertains a woman stranded at the service station with a tale of her first answering machine.

○   ○   ○

MARY LOUISE: I'm gonna whip up some egg salad, you care for some?

[**LEE:** No, thank you.]

MARY LOUISE: Sure? Hostage in a gas station, bound to be hungry. I'm on a high cholesterol diet myself. Lipid center, that's me, two sticks of butter a day. My niece Claudette? She eats macrobiotic; is skinny, pale, got zits, stringy hair and a bad attitude. You ever get squirrely phone calls? Damn, can't get my rings off; look like the Michelin man. First summer I got my answering machine, came home, poured myself a wine cooler, kicked off my shoes and turned to playback. First message: "Mary Louise, I love you." That was the extent. "Mary Louise, I love you." Total stranger, in my dining room. Well. You jump start a battery, that's about how hard my heart kicked in, pounding, full throttle. Scared? I was living alone, still do. Jackson, my third and last – I don't say final – husband, died the year before, prostate cancer, I went round to every room and nailed my windows shut. Lookee here, this one's got a double yolk; twice the cholesterol for the price of one. For weeks, I slept in fear – cold bone-chilling, can't wear your curlers to bed cause they make too much noise on the pillow fear – knife in hand, lying in wait for the laughing slasher, ol' Hannibal the Cannibal. Every day I'd get home from work, ease towards that little red flashing light tells you how many messages. Silvie! You working or waxing your porpoise? Don't want him feeling left out. Never heard from him again. Never did. Every so often, in daylight, I'd rewind the tape, study that voice just in case I ran up against it. Now here's some human nature for you. After a couple of months I began to listen to the message in a whole new light. I started to hear it like maybe that person did truly love me, not in a perverse want to stalk you in your house kill you with a blunt weapon dress up in your skin kind of way, but sincere. Heartfelt. There was passion in his voice, I don't know what your name is if I did I'd say it now. I couldn't help but start to wonder what the man behind the voice looked like, his forearms, his hands. Yeah. I have regretted to this day taping over that message. Haven't heard a man tell me he loved me since. Could be hearing it three times a day. Sure you don't want any egg salad?

STORIES WOMEN TELL
by Janet Overmyer

Mrs. Sims, an angry neighbor, 30-60
Setting: here and now
Serio-Comic

*Mrs. Sims has allowed her dislike of a new neighbor to drive her
to an act of violence.*

O   O   O

MRS. SIMS: Why'd you make me do it? I didn't want to shoot
you. Why did you make me? The mister and me tried to be
good neighbors but you – always laughin' at us, laughin' and
lyin' about us. We heard you, you and your hoity-toity friends!
And spendin' all that money on your houses, makin' us look
bad. We had to put siding on our house, too, and we couldn't
afford it, the mister bein' laid off for so long. Just makin' us
look bad, you didn't even care. And always thinkin' you're so
smart, readin' all them books, when you're dumb, dumb,
dumb! You ain't so smart now, miss, are ya? You and them
dumb cats and your dumb friends and your dumb job. You
ain't no better than us, no better! You and your la-de-da
ways.
   Everybody knows it! Everybody knows what you're like!
Nobody likes you, you know that? Nobody! Why'd you have
to come here, makin' us look bad and talkin' to cats and
feedin' birds and squirrels and just makin' the whole
neighborhood uncomfortable for everybody! We was all fine
till you come. Just a show-off, that's all you are, just a smarty
show-off! Everybody's laughin' at you! Everybody! Nobody
likes you, you know that? Nobody at all, not me, not the
mister, not the Millers, not the Parkinsons, not the
Benedettis, the Hoopers – nobody likes you, nobody wants
you here, why don't you leave, go back where you come
from, why'd you have to come buttin' in here where you ain't
wanted, why'd you have to come here and make me do it?
Why'd you have to make me go and do it?

TOUGH
by George F. Walker

Tina, a young woman facing pregnancy, 19
Setting: a city park, the present
Dramatic

*Tina has confronted her boyfriend about her pregnancy and now
realizes that she will have to go through it alone. Here, she
reveals bitter insight about her future.*

O   O   O

TINA: Remember how hot it was last week? It was really hot.
Anyway, one day last week about four in the afternoon, I saw
a mother and her kid downtown. She was our age. And the
kid was about . . . I don't know – a year. And it was asleep on
her. She was waiting for a bus. I guess they'd been out,
maybe to the doctor, I don't know. But she looked whacked.
The kid was just sprawled over her shoulder. It was sticky hot.
She had a bag full of stuff she was carrying. She looked like
she hadn't slept in weeks, maybe. And the kid is all dead
weight on her. Asleep. But holding her real tight anyway.
She's just standing there like a zombie in that heat holding her
kid and waiting and waiting for that fucking bus. And I knew,
I just knew they were alone. There was just the two of them.
And when they got home there'd still be just the two of them.
Having their supper. Their bath. Going to bed. I mean I
couldn't take my eyes off her and I was feeling, well . . . There
was a great love. A great, great love between them. A bond
. . . tightness. Jesus. You could just feel it. but also . . . well
. . . sadness, eh. Sadness was in the air, too. I mean I don't
know if she was sad or if I was sad from watching her. Maybe
she wasn't sad, maybe she was just so . . . tired she wasn't
feeling anything. Yeah, I don't know, but maybe I was feeling
all these things especially the sadness and she was just so tired
she wasn't feeling anything . . . Not even the love.

TRAPPED DAYLIGHT
by Sharon Houck Ross

Brenna, a woman held captive by her husband, 20-30
Setting: a farmhouse in Kansas
Dramatic

*Brenna's husband has been driven to violence and madness and
has locked her in her room to prevent her from escaping. Here,
Brenna does her best to persuade him to release her.*

○   ○   ○

BRENNA: Wyatt? (*Pause.*) Wyatt, you're not out there making
dinner again, are you? You've been on the tractor all day.
Come on, let me out so I can cook for you.
(*Sound of a box being ripped open.*)
There are other boxes in that cupboard. Corn muffin mix and
tuna. Pork 'n beans.
(*Sound of macaroni pouring into the cold water in the pan.*)
No! Wyatt, remember? The water's got to boil before you put
in the macaroni. It's going to be slimy again.

You know what I could fix tonight? Chicken fried steaks.
That's right. Double-dipped batter with a little garlic salt right
on top, just the way you like it. Cream gravy, Wyatt. And
mashed potatoes. All you have to do is come on over here and
unlock the door.

You know what? I could tell you how to make chicken fries.
I could talk you through it, double batter and all. What do you
way, Wyatt?
(*Clatter of plates and silverware. Brenna slides the magazine
pages under the door, one at a time.*)

BRENNA: Look at this, Wyatt. Henny Penny Chicken Casserole.
(*Another.*) Zucchini Batter Bread, Mile High Biscuits. (*Quickly,
another.*) And pies, pies, Raspberry Twirl, Rhubarb Meringue,
Double Fudge Chocolate Supreme – I've got to have some real
food soon, Wyatt! You didn't come back for lunch today,
remember? Please, please let me out to cook.
(*She takes a metal fingernail file and moves to the window.
She uses the file to pry the screen away from its frame.*)

BRENNA: I said I was sorry. You want me to say it again? I'm sorry, Wyatt. I'm sorry I tried to run away the last time. But that was *one* time. All the other times, I stayed in the house, didn't I? Why don't you think about those times, huh? And let me out for dinner.

I've been praying like you told me and I feel . . . just . . . fine. Very peaceful now. Really. Come see for yourself.
(*She crosses to the door, puts her eye to the keyhole then backs away, straightening her hair and clothing.*)

BRENNA: Wait, wait. Okay, now look. (*Smiling.*) See? Does this look like a . . . violent woman? A sick woman? A woman . . . possessed? Really, Wyatt. Why don't you unlock the door right now and I'll fix chicken fries for us. Then we'll just . . . get on, like we used to, just like before. Just like none of this ever happened. I'm fine now. Promise.

THE VIEW FROM HERE

by Margaret Dulaney

Fern, an agoraphobic, 30s
Setting: a home in suburban Kentucky, the present
Serio-Comic

*Fern has been trapped in her house for many years. Here, she
describes her first bout of agoraphobia.*

O   O   O

FERN: It was just after my 28th birthday that I began my life as a
fruitcake.
(*She pulls herself up to explain.*)
I was out at the Kroger's on Dixie Highway, when it all started.
I'd gone in for a can of tuna and a *Glamour* magazine. I find
the *Glamour* pretty easy, when I notice the linoleum starting
to swim around under my feet. Tried to get a grip on myself.
Figured maybe I just had to focus on what I'd come in for. So I
suck my eyeballs back into my head and head out for the
canned goods. Down, down through the fluorescent
nightmare. Finally, I make it, look over to where the tuna
should be, and it seems they've reorganized their shelves, and
I am staring with horror at a box of Cocoa Puffs. Well, that did
it. – WHAM! – the earth dive-bombed into another part of
space and my shoes weren't sticky enough to hold me on . . . I
head for the exit. Fruit Loops closing in on me. Muzak
throbbing. Grocery carts forming blockades. I pick up my
pace, dodging housewives, tripping over children. I see a giant
toilet paper pyramid in front of me. I hurdle it – stomp on the
rubber stuff, and I'm free . . . Next thing I know, I'm leaning
on the inside of that door there . . . Yeah . . . it was as quiet as
a coffin in here that day.
(*Pause.*)
After a while, I noticed the *Glamour* magazine all scrambled
up in my hands. Now, I have never, ever, ever, stolen one
blessed thing in all my life. Mama used to say, "If you wanna
know what it's like going through life without a rear-end, just
try stealing something." Now, there are two things that I have

never in my life done, and those are – one – steal, and two – eat a booger. So you see, if my behavior in the Kroger's was not enough to convince me that I'd gone mental; the fact that I had run out without paying for that magazine left no room for doubt. I, at the age of 28, out at the Kroger's on Dixie Highway, had slipped into La-La Land.

WATERMELON RINDS

by Regina Taylor

Lottie, a young girl, 14
Setting: here and now
Dramatic

Lottie is a romantic young girl anxiously awaiting her meta-morphosis into womanhood. Here, she longingly contemplates the inevitable change that is to come.

○   ○   ○

LOTTIE: When the hens come home . . .

Sometimes the voices come from outside. My parents. At night I can hear them through the walls. Sometimes I hear the walls quaking, banging. Their voices rise and fall in arias. On the other side. Of the wall. The sheets flapping. Flapping above them. And the beating of bird wings against its bars.

In those mornings I sneak into their room. After they've risen. And search the room. The closets, between the bedcovers . . . searching for signs . . . feathers of the slaughtered birds. Sometimes I find a spot of blood and always the fresh smell of death.

Yang, yang, yang, yang, yang, yang, yang.

When the roosters come home? When the chickens . . . – What Pinkie's baby whispered in my ear . . .

Sometimes the voices come from outside. On the other side. Out there. Like low flying helicopters, their voices. One day – looking out. Three boys talking loud and throwing bottles against the wall. One was black as midnight. One with coiled snakes hissing all over his head. And the third tall and sinewy like a swaying palm. The first one saw me spying and smiled at me. His teeth glistened with gold.

Rapunzel, Rapunzel, let down your golden hair. And he climbed up to her ivory tower . . .

Sometimes the voices come from inside me. Clear as a bell.

She was a poor peasant girl and barely thirteen when she saw the visions and heard the voices that told her to pick up the shield and sword and march to . . . New Orleans?

One day my voices will tell me what and when. My voices will explode. The walls will be knocked down. And you'll see freedom flapping its wings and crowing. When the morning comes.

WHAT A MAN WEIGHS
by Sherry Kramer

Joan, a woman searching for love and beauty, 35
Setting: here and now
Dramatic

Here, Joan shares a favorite daydream.

O   O   O

JOAN: (*In spot, as she places her foot on the first step of the tallest set of stairs – or perhaps the first words are said in darkness, before the spot hits her, already in position.*) I climb the stairs. (*She begins to climb.*) I climb the stairs, and I think – oh yes, he'll be there, he'll be there, and I'll walk through him into another world, and none of the things that make me frightened will ever touch me again, and everything that was ever ugly about me will drop away from me like water. I will be free of it all.

I want to fall down on my knees, I am so goddamn grateful, as I climb the stairs, at the thought of being free, and so I do, in my mind, I fall down on my knees in my mind as I climb the stairs. He is there, and he has freed me from ugliness forever, from the lines around my eyes, the folds beneath my breasts, he has freed me from my thighs, he has freed me from it all. And the longing bucks inside me, and the heat has just kicked in, and I am climbing the stairs, and I am on my knees, and I am so goddamn beautiful, but it's the heat, in the end, that makes me know. That this is true.

Everything else could betray me. Everything else I could just kick aside. But not that heat. That heat doesn't lie, it has never lied, it is my truth, my own, and it does not lie. (*She is at the very top of the stairs, past the landings leading anywhere.*) I have climbed the stairs. And I am filled with him. (*She faces the audience.*)

I love this daydream.

And I hate myself for dreaming it.

I have climbed the stairs. And I am filled with him. (*Beat. She smiles.*) And he isn't there.

WHAT WE DO WITH IT
by Bruce MacDonald

Cheryl, a woman confronting her past, 30s
Setting: here and now
Dramatic

When she was a little girl, Cheryl was abused by her father. After years of denial, she finally confronts him.

O   O   O

CHERYL: What he's doing is a kind of reverse insanity defense, where you claim the victim is crazy. (*To him.*) What did you think? That I would forget? Could you have been so, I don't know, *drunk* that you thought I could forget? (*Beat.*) Or maybe you just convinced yourself it didn't happen because . . . because, otherwise, how could you live with yourself. That was it, wasn't it? You convinced yourself, and you figured I must have done the same thing. (*Beat.*) I read about some of the people who survived the concentration camps. When they first got in, what kept them alive was remembering the lives they had before. But as time went on, and they knew they weren't getting out, they would come to accept the concentration camp as normal, as what life was. They learned how to expect nothing else, they forgot their old life, and so they survived. Are you *lis*tening to this? I came to accept what you did to me as *nor*mal. I've thought about that a lot. In a way it's the hardest thing to live with. Because my thinking it was normal must have helped *you* think it was normal. And I want to be very clear that I am not defending you. I was a child. I was a child. (*Beat.*) About ten years ago I started to remember. Something snapped and . . . I started to remember. It was like finding out I had a serious disease. All of a sudden it was what my life was about.

WOMEN OF THE WILD WEST
by Le Wilhelm

Belle, a saloon girl, 20-30
Setting: the Wild West
Serio-Comic

The Wild West wasn't always kind to women as evidenced in the life story of Belle, a plucky gal who made a career for herself as a saloon singer.

O   O   O

BELLE: My name's Belle. About 50% of all saloon girls are called Belle. I thought I might sing a little ditty for you.
(*She sings something from the 1880's. Not full song, maybe verse, chorus.*)

Now that I've got that out of the way, I'll tell my story. I was born Maude, one of 17 children. Not the first. Not the last. I'm not sure my mother even knew I was around. I was gangly and far from pretty. At the age of 13 when most young girls were starting to get their female shape, nothing happened. And this was a great consternation to me. Even at that age, I knew that breasts on a woman were important. But I wasn't getting any and so I just kept waiting, half afraid that they weren't going to appear. I was fifteen and one half years old. When all of a sudden – "BREASTS."

And I don't mean just breasts, but I mean the most beautiful breasts you ever laid eyes on. Overwhelming! I snuck a piece of cracked mirror out of the house and fixed it in a fork of a cottonwood tree. And every day I'd go there and just stand, looking awestruck. I never got tired of watching them grow. And grow they did. Getting larger and larger. I fell head over heels, utterly and completely in love with my bosom.

They were so beautiful that they brought tears to my eyes, like some people get when they're listening to beautiful music. Milky white, progressing to a vibrant coral. You know, when I think about it, I never really loved anyone or anything else in my entire life as much.

My mother and father arranged for me to get married,

despite my protestations. On my wedding night, I ran away and headed west. Ended up in Dodge City, Kansas, and found myself in a saloon. It was there that I saw what I wanted to be. The women there didn't wear their dresses up high on the necks, they wore them low. And that's what I wanted to do. I wanted to share my treasures with the world. And so I got myself one of them dresses and I put it on and the world agreed with me. The world was thunderstruck by my breasts.

Hanging around a saloon, I learned to sing right good. I travelled around making some good money. But it wasn't my voice that men came to hear. I knew why they were there. Everyone was mesmerized, transfixed by the same thing that had mesmerized me in the cottonwood grove.

It was in a saloon, late at night, in the year 1888, that a man who looked tired and broken asked me if I'd sing "Dixie." It'd been a while since the war, and I thought that it was safe, so I did. (*She sings "Dixie" to "Look away, Dixieland." There is a gun shot.*) It hadn't been long enough. The bullet entered my body right between the eyes. But I died with a smile on my face, 'cause as I was passing out of my earthly flesh, going to the new realm, I heard my killer say, "I could never shoot her in the heart. I could never destroy those beautiful breasts." And if I could have, I'd have kissed him right there. (*Smiling.*) What a way to die. What a way to depart the world.

THE YEARS
by Cindy Lou Johnson

Andrea, a woman ending her marriage, 30-40
Setting: here and now
Dramatic

After 13 years, Andrea has decided to leave her husband. Here, she speaks of the loneliness that drove her to make her decision.

○   ○   ○

ANDREA: I married very young. I just didn't want to be alone. My mother had died that year and I was very lonely.
(*She drifts off.*)
[**BARTHOLOMEW:** I'm sorry.]
ANDREA: The thing is I was much lonelier being married than when I was alone. At least when you're alone you know it, you accept it, but when you're with someone you have expectations that keep being smashed to bits. Over and over . . .
(*She drifts off again.*)
   That's why I left. I just said I needed a little rest, and I got on a plane. But then, when I got there, well, I found this little room to stay in. One side was a plate glass window onto this terrace, and if you were out on the terrace and looked at it, it reflected the sea and the sky and . . . it was very pretty. But then one morning, this bird, this beautiful gull, just smashed into it, and killed himself, because he mistook the reflection for something real, and I thought that's me. That's me. Because when I married I believed there was a journey ahead of me just like he did. I saw this big open sky, just like he did. But it wasn't the sky, it was a reflection. And the beautiful bird he saw flying towards him was himself. And all that beautiful future was just his past. He crashed. He collided with himself. He broke all to pieces . . .

YOUR PLACE OR MINE
by Le Wilhelm

Peggy, a woman who loves to talk, 30s
Setting: an apartment, the present
Serio-Comic

Peggy and Mitch have just met and have chosen to withdraw to Mitch's apartment for a more intimate introduction. Here, Peggy demonstrates her oratory skills as Mitch pours wine.

○　　　○　　　○

PEGGY: I just can't go on a minute longer. I've just got to confess. Just come clean. Put my cards on the table. I feel as if this experience . . . the one between you and me . . . is real deja-vu. No, deja-vu isn't the word I mean, although this experience has some of the ESP feeling that one associates with deja-vu, but deja-vu isn't really it. What I am trying to say, Mitch, albeit not well . . . (*She laughs.*) excuse me, I always laugh when I say albeit. What I'm trying to say is that I feel like a time traveller. That's how you . . . this . . . you and me . . . that's how it all makes me feel. Not forward, but back . . . back to the past . . . like Kathleen Turner in *Peggy Sue Got Married* . . . but not really . . . this is like ten years ago . . . maybe not quite . . . maybe a few years more. But like that. It all started when you looked at me and you said, "Your place or mine?" Right then. I just went zooming into the past. You have no idea how long it has been since someone has said that to me. I mean anyone of any quality. And anyone that I just met . . . that very day. Oh, there have been a few, but you know the types they've been . . . or you can imagine. The types I'd never dream of going with . . . the types that look like they're uncircumcised and don't bathe regularly. That type. I have friends that find that type sexy . . . but I don't. Just not my bag . . . if you get my drift. You do, don't you?

Permissions Acknowledgements